THE
ALTERNATIVE
SCHOOL WITHIN A SCHOOL

Martha Allen
and the students of Drake High School's
SWAS program, 1971-84

BALBOA.
PRESS
A DIVISION OF HAY HOUSE

Balboa Press books may be ordered through booksellers or by contacting:

Balboa Press
A Division of Hay House
1663 Liberty Drive
Bloomington, IN 47403
www.balboapress.com
1 (877) 407-4847

Print information available on the last page.

ISBN: 978-1-5043-6185-9 (sc)
ISBN: 978-1-5043-6186-6 (e)

Balboa Press rev. date: 07/19/2016

INTRODUCTION

This book has been a long time in the making. In June of 2003 I attended a reunion of over a hundred graduates from the alternative high school called SWAS in which I had taught from 1971 to 1984. These former students were now considerably older than I had been when I was their English teacher, but our conversations ignited, and connections were reestablished almost as if no time had passed. Hearing from so many students that day, I came away almost overwhelmed, both by how articulate and successful they were, and also by the realization of just how much their high school experience had shaped their lives and their attitudes. I was the only one of the original teachers still in the classroom, but everyone, former teachers and students alike, voiced strong feelings about the value of the SWAS experience. Two students and I decided we would try to write about our school, and made halting first steps in that direction.

When I turned to the Internet to contact former students five years later, it took only minutes before several dozen had contacted me, wanting to add their voice about what SWAS had meant to them. This book speaks of our experience and of what it can teach us about education today, forty some years later. Organizers of another reunion in the summer of 2010 also used the Internet, with a Facebook page dedicated to SWASies that is still in use. That reunion - and a few, very sad SWAS funerals - brought for me a renewed commitment to this project. Now, we are looking forward to yet another reunion in the summer of 2016.

It was when my daughter just two, just learning to articulate in sentences what she knew of the world around her - "My house is green; Kitty licked me; my Daddy is strong; my Mommy is a teacher" - that I realized how very proud I was of that title: "My Mommy is a teacher." Hearing those words from her made me process that part of my identity in a new way. I was a teacher. I am a teacher. I sometimes think there is no other profession that could possibly satisfy me completely or feel so clearly like "right livelihood." I am a teacher and I love it. I love it still after 36 years of teaching high school English, eight years teaching in a university teaching credential program, and now volunteering at my local elementary school.

I am a good teacher, but there are thousands of excellent teachers in our public schools today. My classroom techniques, my teaching strategies, my command of the curriculum and my rapport with students are no better than countless others'. I am under no illusion that I have anything unique to share in terms of my own teaching. I am writing this book because I believe that I - and my students - do have something to say for we were part of a beautiful and unique educational experiment with many lessons relevant in today's efforts in restructuring schools.

The statistics we see about the realities of our public schools are often disheartening. No Child Left Behind seemed more of a cruel joke than a reality. "No teacher left standing" is what many professionals feel. The gap between wealthy and poorer districts grows wider as budget cuts are made. The new Common Core presents new possibilities for curriculum design, but also real frustration for many teachers.

Teen bullying also appears to have reached epidemic proportions. Gone are the days when it was merely matter of hurt feelings. In Florida, for example, two teens were set on fire by peers over ridiculously minor issues. In another state, a girl was beaten into a coma over a text she sent to another girl that angered that girl's boyfriend. The boyfriend repeatedly kicked the victim in the head, causing brain damage. Cyber-bullying is the high-tech craze, where kids gang up on others using Facebook or other social networks, leading to a number of suicides. Some schools are trying to address the issue, but most schools don't know how to deal with it and, as we've seen all too often in the news, don't react when kids and parents reach out for help.

All of this has an emotional effect on everyone involved. Colleagues talk convincingly about both the lack of professionalism and the lack of respect granted teachers. They lament changing attitudes among students, eroding support from administrators and blatant rudeness from parents frustrated with the system. In addition, teachers simply cannot afford to live in the communities in which they teach, much less think of owning a home. Young, able teachers are leaving the profession for higher paying work. Older, weary teachers talk longingly of retirement.

I do not think it is simple denial or naiveté that makes it impossible for me to embrace this despair. I think I learned something in the thirteen years that I spent teaching in SWAS (School Within a School at Sir Francis Drake High School in San Anselmo, California) that has given me strength, comfort, support and faith - or perhaps stamina is the right word - to go into the classroom with genuine joy every morning.

In addition, current trends in education such as Small Learning Communities, Inquiry-Based Learning, Question-Centered Curriculum, Project-Based Learning, and Problem-Based Learning, all find roots in our SWAS program and other school-within-a-school settings. The Common Core's emphasis on critical thinking and real-world application rings very true to me. My experience in SWAS and primarily with my students during those years has taught me lessons I am certain are important. It is that certainty that leads me to write here, for there are lessons to be found in both our successes and our failures.

In the true spirit of SWAS, no story of our school would be complete without the voices of the students themselves. Therefore, this book is arranged in alternating chapters, the odd numbered ones giving a fairly objective account of the history, the philosophy and the practical structure of our school, but the even numbered ones presenting personal narratives from former SWASies.

TABLE OF CONTENTS

CHAPTER ONE

CHRISTMAS SCHOOL/BEGINNINGS

The teachers agreed that many students were "turned off"
by school, finding it uninteresting and unrelated to their lives.
Further, they agreed that learning could and should
be an exciting and joyful experience.

SWAS STARTED, ALONG WITH many other alternative schools, in the expansive era of the late 1960's when traditional approaches to education were being tested and questioned, and when new priorities and values in education were being set forth. The main difference between SWAS and so many others is that it lasted through the 1970's and well into the 1980's when it found itself with a longer waiting list of students and stronger community support than ever. There were probably two main reasons for this: our willingness to incorporate change into our curriculum, and the closeness and openness with which the staff was able to work. If the school became a family, then the staff was modeling, if not perfect parenting, at least the willingness to listen and to change and a commitment to staying in it for the long run.

Sir Francis Drake High School is a small public school in San Anselmo, California, an upper-middle class town of about 12,000 in Marin County, north of the Golden Gate Bridge. Drake was, and is still, a fine school, with dedicated teachers and a supportive administration in a community that values education. Throughout the McCarthy Era and into the turbulent times of the 60's, the district prided itself of its levelheaded, thoughtful response to controversy. When in 1954, Anne Smart offered the press and the Tam Board of Trustees a list of books she considered subversive, the district refused to cave in to her demand that they be removed. Even after she convinced the Grand Jury that "someone at a higher level" had deliberately recommended these books "to plant seeds of Communism" in the minds of the district's children, the Board of Education insisted that they examine each book in detail and concluded that each one should remain on the curriculum. (Louise S. Robbins: Censorship and the American Library)

By the time of the late 60's, the same rebellious spirit that had ignited the Berkeley campus just across the bay had found expression within the Tam District as well. One boy whose "Fuck the Draft" button had gotten him expelled took his case all the way to the state's highest court.

Surprisingly perhaps, most controversial of all was the debate about the length of hair allowed on school athletes. Athletic director Bob Troppman suggested a rule requiring that hair shouldn't come over the collar or the ears. According to Troppmann, there was an overwhelming vote in favor of the restriction. Then came track season, when several students didn't want to get haircuts. According to Doug Basham, track and cross-country coach at the time, some students wore their hair long to display their views on the Vietnam War. "It seemed as though the people that were pro Vietnam War were always the militarists who had short hair, and those that were not were sort of the ones that were described as hippies of some sort," said Basham. "It's never that black and white, but that's the way it became." Basham chose to back up his track athletes, who wanted to wear longer hair than the rules allowed, but five athletes ultimately were not allowed to participate in track that season because they would not follow the rules.

When these students insisted on taking the matter to the school board, seven hundred community members, on both sides, attended a board meeting in the gym to debate the issue of hair length. After hearing all of the debate and questions, the board voted 3-2 in favor of keeping the short hair policy. Two of the runners took their case to court, saying that their personal rights had been violated. Basham and lawyers backed up the students. In 1970, the case was brought to the district court in San Francisco as Neuhaus v. The Tamalpais Union High School District. When the testimonies were finished, the judge ruled in favor of the athletic department, saying they could determine whatever rules they want. However, according to Basham, the district eventually allowed coaches to set standards for their own teams. (The Redwood Bark Online http://redwoodbark.org)

Against this backdrop, the Tamalpais Union High School District was encouraged to expand alternatives in what was acknowledged to be a top-ranked district. A 1969 report to the Board of Trustees prepared by a study committee stated: "We would recommend the provision of a greater variety of learning situations to meet the wide diversity of individual student needs, such as the further development of alternative school environments and styles open to all parents, students and teachers."

At Drake, a dedicated group of teachers and students would meet in Room 219 to discuss what an alternative school environment might look like. The Social Studies department, under Duane Miller, arranged to have that classroom open all day, and it became the center of on-going conversation and argument about just what school should be. Students painted a mural on the back wall and the room was furnished with rugs and sofas, actions which attracted considerable controversy. Perhaps most importantly, Room 219 housed a large paperback library of the many books published at the time about education. Jackie Moskowitz, one of the most actively involved teachers remembers it this way: "It was truly bottom-up. It is a rare thing to have this kind of reform. In fact, it was a most radical process: the discussion, the thinking, the talking about education." Marny Sorgen, a math teacher who was equally important to the formation of this group said, "It was the students who insisted that this had to lead to something, not be just talk." Those who had found a home in Room 219, joined by another group of teachers who had been meeting in the office behind science teacher Rudy Genetti's room, went to the principal, Harold Allison, who urged them to do more.

A 1970 report from Drake High School's Committee on Educational Environment recommended that the district move toward a program "in which alternative school environments and styles are open to all parents, students and teachers." That same year, the School Studies Workshop report had asked "How and what shall our students learn in order to best prepare them to cope with their 'expanding' society and prevent them from going into 'future shock'? ...To be effective today, schools and teachers must encourage students to discover their own capacities for learning, for creativity, and the ability to adapt to change."

Tam District teachers were certainly not alone in reexamining educational policy and the structure of schools. There were a number of important precedents. A.S. Neill's school in England called Summerhill provided an exciting, if controversial model of progressive education. "The function of the child is to live his own life – not the life that his anxious parents think he should live, not a life according to the purpose of the educator who thinks he knows best," he wrote. His bestselling book by the same name (1960) had ignited the field of educational philosophy, challenging traditional, authoritarian classrooms. His idea that children can be trusted with a desire to learn, that "freedom works" turned the field of education upside down. Their school's policy statement describes their school as a place "where kids have freedom to be themselves ... and success is not defined by academic achievement but by the child's own definition of success." Furthermore, Neill's Summerhill was not just a theory: the school had been successfully running for 40 years.

Ivan Illich in his startling book, *Deschooling Society*, (1971) decried the "increasingly mechanized, industrialized and dehumanizing" educational system. He called for a cultural revolution urging us to "abolish schooling" altogether. Herbert Kohl's *The Open Classroom: A practical guide to a new way of teaching.* proved to be a manual for teachers who "want to teach in non-authoritarian ways… dispense with textbooks and find more interesting alternatives, to work together with students to develop a sense of community with young people which extends beyond the classroom." (p. 14-16).

John Holt's *How Children Learn*, (1960) also examined our educational system, using anecdotal observations and calling for a more sensitive and intimate relationship between teacher and student. Holt believed children were born both teachers and learners, that they want to solve problems if teachers and parents would only get out of the way. Holt also emphasized the importance of self-esteem for children's learning. His *Freedom and Beyond* (1972) would go even further, denouncing the competition inherent in school sports and calling for schools where students are given free choice about what is important to them to learn.

Amid this backdrop, the Room 219 teachers and students conceived of the idea of a "Christmas School," with optional classes offered during three days of the two week winter break in 1969-70, in which teachers and students could determine the kind of material they thought most relevant. The project was designed with only three basic principles in mind: that participation be completely voluntary; that the student-teacher ratio be no more than ten to one; and that adults and young people be seen as equals as teachers and learners. With no pre-planned activities, the curriculum would be developed on the basis of interest and the nature of the participants.

Ten volunteer teachers and approximately 140 students began the three-day experiment by responding to the following questions:

1. What questions do you feel are worth answering?
2. Why are you here? What do you expect to get out of this?
3. What do you have to offer?

On the basis of these responses, activity and interest groups were organized. One group examined the work of Vietnamese poets, another went on field trips to study marine biology and yet another went into San Francisco for experiments in talking with people, strangers. Other groups explored ceramics, cooking, dance, space and the future, human relationships - all things the students themselves wanted to know about. The Room 219 group met in the Little Theater. "We teachers did little talking. We'd sit in a circle on the stage and raise questions and the students would take it from there," recalls Sorgen. Discussions grew and gained momentum during Christmas School, focusing on the topic of philosophy of education, and more specifically on the problems and potential for the students' own education. They examined the possibility of creating a "School Within a School" on the Drake campus. This initial group of teachers and students wanted a small school community in which new ways to learn could be tried, and in which students could take more responsibility for their own education. They wanted a school in which knowledge was seen as unified rather than fragmented by subject classification, and the goal of education was recognized as considering the human's total scope, rather than just intellectual activities.

Students and teachers alike wanted to maintain the enthusiasm and positive learning found during this vacation period during the rest of the school year. The Christmas School ended with an enormous banquet that was conceived, planned and prepared entirely by the cooking group. Enthusiasm was high.

From these discussions about how to keep this learning environment alive once school started again in January came a committee that met regularly all the following spring. Now calling themselves the SWAS (School Within a School) group, they submitted a preliminary proposal to the Research and Development Council of the school, which granted funds to facilitate further and more detailed planning. "To have so many students and teachers willingly attend school during Christmas vacation was one thing, but then to have the discussions extend beyond that experiment took real dedication," said Moskowitz. "Again, it was the students who insisted we had to *do* something, not just talk."

In line with current educational planning models, the group came up with a statement of philosophy and several goals and objectives.

They found many current books to support their quest. The wording of their final statement reflects the times and the optimistic philosophy of Charles E. Silberman's *Crisis in the Classroom*, George Leonard's *Education and Ecstasy*, (which The San Francisco Examiner called "perhaps the most important book on schools, their problems and their potential written in this generation") William Glasser's *Schools Without Failure* and Postman and Weingartner's *Teaching as a Subversive Activity*.

While the Tamalpais Union High School District was clearly one of the best in the state, and perhaps the country, teachers recognized the truth of Bob Dylan's words: "The times they were a-changin'." Having heard speakers such as Richard Suchman and William Glasser present challenging ideas about the future of education, teachers were encouraged to look for substantial change in the educational model.

These influences, added to the personal frustrations about teaching experienced by some of the staff, fueled this group to keep meeting, keep searching for answers. The teachers agreed that many of their own students were "turned off" by traditional school, finding the curriculum uninteresting and unrelated to their lives. Further, they agreed that learning could and should be an exciting and joyful experience. They saw that both teachers and students needed to change in order to make school more meaningful. By late spring, this SWAS group submitted a preliminary proposal for an alternative school to be housed with Drake High School. The proposal started with this paragraph:

> *In our young people lies much of the hope for the future of this society.*
>
> *In the brief exposure these people have to the high school program, it is critical that the best job be done to prepare them for the largely unknown demands of the future. Our premise is that school should move these*
>
> *people toward becoming independent learners who will know their own goals and needs, who will teach as well as learn, and who will discover the joy of learning and teaching.*

The committee submitted a list of assumptions about people (it was important that the philosophy center on beliefs about "people," and not just "students") and learning:

1. *People are curious and have a natural potentiality for learning;*
2. *Learning can and should be a joyous experience;*
3. *Active learning is better than passive learning;*
4. *Learning is most effective when it allows the student to enhance his self-concept and, therefore, to develop his own ethic;*
5. *Learning is most pervasive and lasting when it involves the whole person and not just his intellect;*
6. *A person must know how to learn and be open to experience and change if he is to be most useful to himself and his society;*
7. *Reality is better perceived when it is not arbitrarily subdivided or compartmentalized.*
8. *Random learning is as fruitful as learning which follows imposed, logical progression;*
9. *Learning is most effective when the student believes the subject and the learning activities it involves have relevance for him;*
10. *Learning is maximized when the learner determines his own directions, helps discover his own resources, formulates his own problems and questions, decides his course of actions, sets his own standards, and lives with the consequences of his choices;*
11. *Learning is enhanced by sharing learning experiences with others;*
12. *Teaching is an important method of learning.*

Using these assumptions, the committee developed the goals focused on helping each student and teacher to:

1. *develop a better understanding of himself;*
2. *find a well-founded self-confidence;*
3. *develop a greater sense of personal and community responsibility*
4. *learn how to learn;*
5. *determine his own direction, discover his own resources, identify his own problems, and formulate their solutions;*
6. *evaluate his own performance;*
7. *learn how to cope with change;*
8. *learn how to live in a pluralistic society;*
9. *learn how to create an environment where learning takes place under pleasant and enticing circumstances;*

10. *find learning experiences that involve the whole person, not merely the intellect.*

The goals were admirable, if vague. Today it may be easy to view them with a certain cynicism - or perhaps with a nostalgia for the times. However, I believe that they were, in fact, met by the SWAS program. Do we have data to support that we succeeded in helping a student "determine his own direction, discover his own resources, identify his own problems, and formulate their solutions"? Of course not. But can we show that each student did, in fact, "evaluate his own performance"? Yes. And we have anecdotal evidence that even the loftiest and most impossible to measure goals, such as learning "how to create an environment where learning takes place under pleasant and enticing circumstances," were met time and time again. Also, it is worth noting that, in hindsight, one can find the seeds of our best successes and also the reason for some of our most persistent problems. Those problems will be discussed in later chapters.

In line with the educational model of the era, the "objectives" were - in theory at least - more easily measured or observed than the more general "goals". The SWAS committee listed only four objectives:

1. *to improve the self-image of each student*
2. *to improve the students' attitude toward learning and toward school*
3. *to improve the students' attendance records*
4. *to improve the students' competence in academic skills.*

These objectives were measured at the end of the two-year trial program. A thorough report was presented to the Board of Education at that time. No further special funding was asked for or received, but the SWAS program was well established and continued for eleven more years. But I jump ahead. First the teachers had to be selected.

The SWAS committee agreed that a SWAS teacher needed to be someone who believed in the philosophy as stated in the proposal and was able to deal openly and honestly with other staff members, appreciating the closeness that would be essential among teachers and between teachers and students. They came up with a page-long description of the qualities necessary for a good teacher, which included the ability to be versatile, tolerant, sensitive, and which ended - perhaps as a reflection of the end of the committee's tolerance with current edu-speak - with the requirement that he or she be a "good crap detector" and be "beautiful."

Perhaps most prophetic of all, the list included the requirement that the teacher "be willing to spend the extra time necessary to get the program started (should not be heavily committed to other projects and activities requiring after-school meetings)." The group agreed that teachers must be able to make at least a two-year commitment to the program; ironically, both Marny Sorgen and Jackie Moskowitz were just starting families and felt - despite all their efforts to get SWAS off the ground - that they could not make this time commitment.

The work of this SWAS committee concluded in February of 1971 with the selection of five teachers - despite these rather overwhelming requirements - and plans to gain approval for a pilot program to begin in September of 1971. It is probably worth noting the dollar amounts asked for and received: $340 for each of the five teachers and $500 for consultants, both professionals and students.

The next task for this group was to translate the work of the original SWAS committee into specific policies and procedures. An entire school's operation had to be constructed from the philosophical base that they had established. By May, a report was sent to the Research and Development Council and a summer workshop was planned for the five teachers and a handful of students. By the close of the school year, they had plans in hand for the first year of a new alternative school, as well as a list of over a hundred interested students.

CHAPTER TWO

THE FIRST YEAR: CHRIS FULMER AND BOB MORGEN

Whoever thought it was a good idea to let squirrelly adolescents design their own curriculum wasn't completely nuts.

Much to everyone's surprise at Drake, some of us managed to get rather conventional educations at SWAS. I studied Trigonometry and Analytic Geometry [which] taught me enough Calculus to pass the AP math test.

Why would students leave the main campus to join a start-up experimental school? Could student-defined curriculum succeed? What was it like to be a student in a radically new environment? Two former students answer these questions. Not surprisingly, the answers are very personal and specific to individual circumstances, but common themes emerge.

CHRIS FULMER: IT'S RARE when you can look back and recognize the exact moment when your entire life changed. My life-altering event at SWAS? A moment of blazing clarity when I understood that my life was my own, and that I could shape my own destiny. It came when I collaborated with other students, SWAS instructors, and a teacher at the main high school to start an electronics class. I already had a passion for figuring out how things worked. What I didn't know was that the SWAS electronics class was going to light a fire in me academically.

The first day of the course I was very excited but also nervous. After all, we'd pulled a lot of favors from the faculty to kick this off and I wanted the plan to succeed, and I wanted to succeed, as well. The instructor started off as expected, describing the coursework, but then he did something that really opened my eyes. He painted a picture of a career in electronics. Wake up in the morning and create a new product, or a new concept. Even something that could change the world. Was I thinking too big? No. As eloquently painted by the teacher, I saw a clear picture of what my life could be someday.

The electronics course reinvigorated my passion for learning. I was transformed that day and I've never looked back. I went on to earn an AS at College of Marin studying electronics, and worked as an electronics technician for several years while completing a BSEE in electrical engineering computer science at UC Berkeley. Whenever I'm back in Marin County and drive past Sir Francis Drake High School, I feel a special appreciation for the SWAS teachers and administrators back in the day. Whoever thought it was a good idea to let squirrelly adolescents design their own curriculum wasn't completely nuts.

While SWAS transformed my academic enthusiasm, it also took my social life from grim to great. I'd struggled in the main high school, and in fact had received my first (and only) failing grade - in P.E. - before entering SWAS. After the coach looked on while a bunch of jocks stripped off half my clothes and threw me into the girls' gym, I never once attended his class again. Really, they should have been nicer to me. I was on the verge of a growth spurt that would shock my parents and give me a "wingspan" of almost seven feet, which turned out to be very handy on the volleyball court.

Fortunately, the atmosphere in SWAS was much more inclusive. The strangest, most wonderful things could happen, like when I found myself appointed to the social committee, planning parties and other events just for our group. What, me? Yes, awkward, gear-geeky me. Every so often, I pull out a stack of old albums and listen to the soundtrack of my life in high school: Badfinger's "No Dice"; Grateful Dead's "American Beauty"; Cat Stevens' "Teaser and the Firecat". As soon as I drop the needle in the groove, the years rewind, and I find myself back at SWAS, setting up the sound system for a school-sponsored party with fellow audiophiles Randy and Kyle. Among Randy's collection of high fidelity gear, I envied a pair of very sweet Golden Ear speakers as well as his Marantz 8B power amplifier and Acoustic Research turntable. I was pretty proud of my own Dynaco PAT-4 pre-amplifier and ST70 power amplifier. Some of that equipment has stood the test of time...I still use it. Randy's broad and sophisticated musical tastes ranged from rock to jazz, making him our playlist authority. It was Kyle, now a great musician in his own right, who introduced me to the Grateful Dead, who talked me out of buying more Bread albums, and who helped me understand that my musical tastes could not in any way be considered cool. There was a lot at stake with those party playlists. We felt that the success of the whole party rested on our adolescent shoulders. It was crucial to pick the right songs, and critical to play them in the right order. The three of us held long meetings to debate which songs to include as we compiled the list. Good dance tunes to get the party rocking, a wide selection of artists to reflect the diverse audience, and then, as the night went on, slow dance songs to bring couples together. After more than four decades, I only have flashes of memories: images of the audio equipment set up in one main room; couches, chairs, and bean bags crowded against the walls; couples spilled out into the hallways, dancing, flirting, talking, kissing. After all, how could all of us fit into one classroom during these parties? Was there food? Was there a theme or decorations? Surely there must have been chaperones—teachers working unpaid overtime, watching sweaty, hormonal teens fumble their way to adulthood—but I don't remember these details any more.

What I do remember is the feeling of intense excitement. Yes, it was only a high school party, but being a part of the planning—planning on our terms—made me feel like I belonged. It didn't matter whether we were geeky or shy or uncool, or whether we were a social outcast by Drake standards. In SWAS, we all seemed to fit in, and the parties somehow proved that to me. They were just silly parties, but they gave me a level of confidence that's stood the test of time. Just like my old audio gear.

Chris Fulmer has worked as an aerospace engineer at Hughes Aircraft Company, General Dynamics, and NASA. More recently he's worked with consumer electronics at General Instrument, Motorola, and Google. Chris is currently an electrical engineering consultant living in Southern California.

Bob Morgen, a student leader that first year who also took part in planning the program, also remembers the parties and celebrations. He shared some other very specific memories: There were the feasts; one was Thanksgiving where we cooked roast turkey for 150 people. Where did we get the money? I remember using the Home Ec kitchens, but I don't recall organizing the actual cooks. Yet I feel like I did, which might be a false memory. More likely I just forgot. Another feast was Cornish game hens. I think that one was smaller - like 100 people. But it was historically remarkable because I brought in bottles of cheap Cointreau to make the orange sauce for the hens, and also to flavor the chocolate mousse. The teachers who helped with that are now likely dead, so I can reveal this without fear that they will be arrested for contributing to the delinquency of a minor. Things were different then ...

The feasts helped me get my first real job. Paul Ehrlich was part of a small commune that owned a restaurant, "The Wild Mountain Café" in Larkspur. I worked there the summer after my senior year as the cook. Paul figured that if I could make turkey dinner for 150, I could make guacamole tacos at his small restaurant. So at barely 18 years old, with only SWAS training, I was on my own by day two, cooking lunches for the likes of Leigh French and David Crosby.

I also remember a very kind teacher named Karen Emmons. She was beautiful and bright. I wonder how old she was then? Thirty, maybe? Karen would bring in an artichoke for her lunch and eat it with me and Patsy, who was my best friend. Patsy had a tough life - her family was confusing but I found Patsy one of the most fun, creative, thoughtful, and lovely people of my teenage years. Karen would eat all the leaves off her artichoke and she was done. Thin people are like that. They just suddenly stop eating even though there is more! Then Karen would offer the artichoke heart to me and Patsy to split, which we did greedily. If I'm ever asked to testify at Karen's canonization, I would site these saintly acts of lunchtime generosity.

Another Karen memory comes from even before the first year of SWAS. There were, in some disciplines, more teachers who wanted to be in SWAS than there were openings. In English there was Eliene Bundy, who had been much involved in the organizing, and Karen Emmons, who, if I recall correctly, had not been. Eliene was about 50 years old then, which seemed ancient to us. To decide which English teacher to accept into year one of SWAS, we had a vote. I am still astonished that we teenagers were given an equal voice with the teachers in that vote. To my surprise, the teachers all voted for Karen over Eliene. Eliene looked very disappointed, almost bitter when she was told, and I remember her muttering something about how young Karen was and how that was the real reason. This is a very old memory, and may involve significant projection on my part, but it is one of my oldest memories of professional disappointment - and thus a memory that I treasure and go back to often. I remember being delighted when Eliene got the opportunity to join SWAS in year two after Karen went off to Thailand.

Much to everyone's surprise at Drake, some of us managed to get rather conventional educations at SWAS. I studied Trigonometry and

Analytic Geometry with Chris, who then taught me enough Calculus to pass the AP math test. The extra AP credits gave me a lot of flexibility and I was able to do two majors at UC: philosophy and mathematics. It was quite a luxury and privilege to be able to study philosophy, yet to do something that would get you a job as well! Back in the middle of the last century, an MA in Mathematics was a sufficient credential to get a job as a computer programmer, which I did at SRI. These days we now have Computer Science departments. Not then. It was Chris who taught me to program. She would have us write a short computer program, in pencil, and she would keypunch it onto cards at the district office then run it on the district's computer. She would bet us 25¢ that our program wouldn't run because of a syntax error. She actually kept the money. She made a fortune!

In fact, Chris is the teacher I remember most fondly. She always seemed to be up to something just slightly inappropriate; always playing a long con. Her dry wit was an inspiration to me. And while I loved mathematics before I met her, she was the one who showed me the day-to-day business of mathematics. We would approach a hard problem together, one that she clearly didn't 'just know' the answer to. And with facial expressions and raised eyebrows, she would communicate that it was going to make our brains hurt if we attacked this problem. And then we did.

Other things would have upset the larger school community, I'm sure. I have a vague recollection of a lecture by a guy from Morehouse, an experimental community was founded on the "More Philosophy" in which their working premise was that people and things are right the way they are and include the potential for change. Again, the teacher who arranged that would be in jail today since Morehouse was basically a sex commune, or at least one might be forgiven for thinking so. Tall, slender, handsome young Tom Carey sat cross-legged during the lecture with one of his willowy blond girlfriends attached to him. The lecturer pointed at Tom and told him that he was the "New Age" version of the traditional high school football hero who got all the girls. I believe we giggled. Tom, in the end, got the best girl of them all, Janet Leigh, who is a bestselling author of novels for teens. Tom himself also managed to get educated and ended up with a career as a developer at Microsoft, aka The Evil Empire, for which we can't blame SWAS. Anyway, he has a Mac now.

Then there is the fact that my senior prom date and I went in drag,

I in a dress and she is a tux. We were greeted politely at the door, but no doubt we fueled more rumors about those crazy SWASies.

> *After college Bob got a job at the Stanford Research Institute, working first as a programmer and later in applied artificial intelligence and speech recognition. In 1997 he moved to London where he works in business development while enjoying gourmet cooking and the good life.*

CHAPTER THREE

QUESTION-CENTERED CURRICULUM AND THE BLOCK SCHEDULE

Teachers wanted students to ponder "What is civilization?" while
students' questions were closer to "Where can we go today?"
and "How long can we stay there?"

I'll never forget the joke:
How many SWASies does it take to change a lightbulb?
10 - one to change it and nine to figure out how to get credit for it.

HESE ACCOUNTS BY TWO students, so active in the first year, underscore three essential philosophical ideas, which when braided together, formed the foundation for SWAS. First, the most fundamental assumption upon which the new school was formed was that although there were many students who move comfortably and with great benefit through a modern high school, there were also many others who found it a lonely world in which it was difficult for them to find connection with teachers or other students. Some also found that because of a public high school's size and relative fixed routines, they could not easily adapt it to their individual pace and interests. They needed a small school, where students and teachers could spend more time together, where there could be greater informality, and where projects could be tailored for individual student needs, without disrupting the planning of the larger school.

The second idea was that an essential purpose of the SWAS program was to break down the rigid separation of disciplines by devising a topical organization of the curriculum to replace the subject matter organization. They planned to introduce a greater use of the "real" world as a learning place, to move the school out of the confines of the school building or campus, in order to tap into the vitality of the world at large.

These two assumptions: the need for deeper and more meaningful connections among students and teachers, students and students, and students and their education; and the view that education must move beyond the borders of the school shaped the initial planning for the program and remained core beliefs throughout the thirteen years of the SWAS program.

In planning the first year, however, a third assumption also shaped the curriculum planning. Idealism - and perhaps naiveté - dominated all suggestions about what should be taught. It was decided that the entire school would be based on a question-centered study, designed to provide students with the opportunity to explore an area of vital interest and, in the process, to satisfy the requirements of the existing school curriculum. We would begin by simply asking: "What questions are worth answering?" Through brainstorming, analyzing synthesizing and integrating, students and teachers were to compile a list of questions to be investigated. Students, then, would decide which questions interested them the most through conferences with teachers and discussions with other students. It was hoped that natural groupings would occur, and the methods of approach selected by each group. The entire Question-Centered Curriculum proposal can certainly be seen as a forerunner to Theodore Sizer's work and to the current emphasis on Inquiry-Based Learning.

Ken Genetti remembered everyone being crammed into one room at the very beginning of the year, and the teachers asking "What do you guys want to do?" The meeting was then turned over to a senior, Brad Rippee, who "went to the blackboard and wrote 'Question-Centered Curriculum' and then he wrote all these question marks all over the board. He said we should come up with the questions and then we will come up with a curriculum based on what you guys want to learn."

Students did succeed in generating several "big" questions and then began the process of organization into study teams. Many students, however, began to ask, " Yes, fine, but how do I get math credit?" Both students and teachers began to suffer anxiety about the amount of time this was taking and felt uncomfortable "doing nothing." Tolerance for ambiguity may have been one of the qualities cited as necessary for a successful SWAS teacher, but ambiguity proved a more powerful opponent than anyone had anticipated.

To relieve the anxiety, the entire school decided that subject matter classes should begin immediately, and that questions could evolve from them. The start of classes met immediate needs, were comfortable for everyone involved, provided a sense of accomplishment, and therefore never led back to an in-depth exploration of the big questions.

Some of the ideas of the question-centered curriculum did pass on to the operation of classes, however. Students worked on a contract basis with teachers, and worked together to decide on methods of study, the scope and detail to the work, and the amount of time needed to meet the requirements. Teachers were seen as both counselors and experts in their fields. It was the teachers' responsibility to give credit for students' work; evaluations were reached through individual conferences. Although at first it was accepted that no grades were to be given at SWAS and the teachers were comfortable with this, the students quickly seemed to want the security of having a letter grade assigned to their work. At first, credit and grades were negotiated between each student and teacher. A sort of wagering ("How about you give me three units of A rather than 5 units of C?") became common, and here it was the teachers who were uncomfortable, and searched for the security of a more clearly defined plan.

Looking back, the first year seems to have been a time of very sincere trial and error, with as many failures as successes. It is to the credit of both staff and students that the program kept going despite the failures, and learned lessons with each one. In the spring of the first year, the staff, having abandoned the idea of students generating a question-based curriculum, but still convinced the idea itself was a solid one, designed one on their own. The entire school was organized into small teams and given the task of designing a "Survival City" for ten thousand people. The idea was that the scope of the project would force students to use all the disciplines. They were to include physical design, social organization, and ecological needs. As the teams found need for more information, classes were to be formed.

This may have been one of the most ill-advised decisions the staff ever made. After initial enthusiasm, the students became disillusioned by the magnitude of the task and their inability to work well in groups. When compromises could not be reached, the groups splintered into smaller ones, which only complicated the immensity of the task. Again anxiety about "regular" courses arose. "What about French credit?" Students began to resent being forced to participate in a project, a staff idea, while their other courses were seemingly ignored.

We developed a motto that was to remain essential to the SWAS philosophy: "Never everyone." It was clear that we could not expect any one process, structure or idea, no matter how seemingly open-ended, to meet the needs of every student. While we forgot this lesson from time to time, and tried to institute other school-wide programs, we gradually learned not to try to force a one-size-fits-all approach about anything.

Survival City ended at this point. A few students who had become genuinely involved continued their study until the end of the semester, but most returned to a schedule of regular classes. Not that the schedule we created was very regular. With a college schedule of classes meeting on alternate days, students were faced with figuring out if it were an "A Day" or a B Day" or perhaps a "Special Wednesday" when there would be field trips. The students and teacher determined course length, the amount of credit given negotiated.

Throughout the first year, attempts were made to provide time for students to engage in different learning activities away from the school campus. In May of the first year, all classes were suspended for a week so that the students and staff could participate in extended field trips or individual projects. We called this project On-Location. While the staff generated a variety of suggestions to stimulate student thinking, it was ultimately the students' responsibility to submit their own plans for the week. For those with definite, concrete ideas for projects, the week was a great success.

However, many students and staff members found that commitments to the regular Drake classes (such as chemistry, which was not offered at SWAS, for example) precluded participation in on-location activities. For still more, the week seemed disconnected from their regular class work. Some resented this imposed interruptions to their regular classes. Once again, the lesson seemed to be that we could not force the entire school population to enjoy - or even to participate in - any one project or idea.

Throughout the first year and into the second, other attempts were made to provide students time to engage in different learning activities away from campus. Some were classes such as Twentieth Century Art in which staff took a group of students to museums and artists' studios in San Francisco and Marin. Other attempts centered on using one day a week ("Weird Wednesdays" and then later two half-days on Tuesdays and Thursdays) for off-campus learning. With only six staff members and limited transportation, however, it was impossible to schedule a sufficient number of field trips to involve everyone. Unfortunately "field trips" came to mean free time to too many. The teachers at Drake High School began to have legitimate complaints about our students "hanging out" on Wednesdays; perhaps more importantly, our own students began to feel they were drifting, with no real purpose.

In retrospect, it seems as if our concept of an "alternative school" was fairly limited. Teachers dreamed of an idealized question-based curriculum where motivated students generated exciting curriculum ideas and managed to earn subject-matter credit while answering broad, philosophical questions about the nature of man. For students, on the other hand, the key phrase was the "real world"; their greatest desire was to learn about this real world, and the main motivation was to get as far outside the four walls of the school building as possible. Teachers wanted students to ponder "What is civilization?" while students' questions were closer to "Where can we go today?" and "How long can we stay there?"

There were many positives as well; the list of mini-courses taught was impressive:

Marine Biology, Coastal Workshop, Astrology, Dance, Calligraphy, Computers, Slide Rule, Genetics, Shakespeare, Justice in America, Gourmet Cooking, Critical Thinking, Nutrition, Electricity and Electronics, Ancient Literature, Wilderness Survival, Video. German, Faulkner, Steinbeck, etc There were also on-going courses in French, Spanish, math and writing. A list of the field trips included outings to the Bay Model, Exploratorium, Sufi Dancing, Audubon Canyon Ranch, Point

Reyes Seashore, Tomales Bay, Joshua Tree, as well as regular trips to local museums, lectures and plays at Dominican College and College of Marin.

SWAS entered the second year with enormous enthusiasm and pride in what we had been able to do. SWASies as we came to call ourselves, students and teachers alike, had already gained a reputation and a self-image. (We tried several times to come up with another, better name for the program, thinking SWAS would just be temporary, but nothing else seemed to stick, so SWAS we were and SWAS we remained.) Part of the self-image, it must be admitted, was a certain pride in what SWASies perceived to be their bad reputation with the larger school. Yes, there were Drake teachers who worried about long-haired kids who seemed to play volleyball all morning, and there were Drake students who thought that their SWAS friends were always headed to the beach, but SWASies were proud of their different-ness and were sure we were on the verge of discovering important things about education.

It should be noted that we attracted a wonderful collection of kids in the first years of our program. Perhaps the average hair length was longer than that of the main campus, and undoubtedly we attracted students who did not fit in with the accepted stereotypes of 1970's teens or of their peers on the main campus. We had the first computer geeks, we had children of beatnik poets and painters, we had shy loners, and we had incredibly motivated student leaders whose articulate expression of what they felt school should and could be was awe-inspiring. Overall, we had a wonderful mix of individuals who might never have been friends in a regular school, but who bonded over the goal of making SWAS work.

It's important to remember that in the first years of SWAS, Nixon was still president, we were at war in Vietnam and there was a draft. The larger world held perils and our small community was intent on making a safe and welcoming environment.

CHAPTER FOUR

THE SECOND YEAR: JULI GICKER

I no longer wanted to stand out in a crowd;
I needed to belong to one. SWAS was exactly that –
a crowd of unique people.

I CAME FROM A VERY politically liberal family, living in a very politically conservative community. Marin County was once described to me as a community that may vote for liberal candidates or programs, but isn't willing to put its money where its mouth is. When Cyra McFadden wrote *The Serial*, first published in our local free press weekly newspaper that also featured Dr. Hip and Dag's Bag, I felt that I had found a kindred spirit; she saw the same hypocrisy I did. As a young person, I always felt there was something wrong with the community I lived in. I was angry and I was searching.

My family constantly seemed to be having political confrontations with other people. While watching coverage of the assassination of Robert Kennedy at a friend's house, her father came in and announced, "Turn that son of a bitch Catholic off!" and proceeded to announce, "You're a goddamn Catholic, too!" I wasn't, but certain in his knowledge that I was somehow different, he kicked me out of his house anyway.

People called my family "hippies" because my brother wore long hair. Bullying was a peripheral issue for my whole family. When a classmate of my brother's was beaten so badly that he suffered a split spleen simply because his hair was long, my world changed; another was expelled from middle school because he refused to cut his hair. My parents assumed my brother Randy would be next and discussed how we would handle it, but the issue was resolved before anything happened. Meanwhile, my oldest brother was strip-searched going through customs because his long hair and a gold watch he had inherited from his grandfather made the officials feel he was a drug dealer. The world was not a safe place for really stupid reasons.

The political climate of the 60's and 70's kept conversations around the dinner table very lively. Our ideals and principles made us somehow different. I wasn't sure why, but I knew it was "us against them." However, the comfort and shelter of my family provided me with a good sense of myself and my friends accepted me for the renegade I was.

I went to the main school for my first year at Drake High School, and I was miserable. Rich kids driving their parents' expensive sports cars, concerned about clothing and appearances and being intolerant of anyone else were more than I could take. At the beginning of my sophomore year, I simply decided I was no longer going to go to school. The only class I liked was public speaking. Fortunately for my plan, it was held first period. I would get up early with my family, go to my first period class, and then cut school for the rest of the day. The next day I would bring in a note which said, "Please excuse Juliann for missing school yesterday ..." forged with my mother's signature. After almost three full weeks, the phone rang at our house one evening. It was a counselor from school asking my mother if she had written excuses for me. My parents and I had a long discussion after that.

Coming from a debate-loving family such as mine, I had learned very early how to speak for myself and sound convincing, and more confident than I felt. Calls must have been made on my behalf, for despite having heard that there was a waiting list for sophomore girls wanting to enter the SWAS program, I soon got a note in my first period class that I had been accepted to that program. The teacher read the note aloud to the class, and was greeted with a chorus of "Oh, nooo!" and "Wow, I thought you were okay" and "SWASies are a bunch of losers," etc. I suspect that many of us had bullying issues or fear-of-bullying issues prior to coming to SWAS.

I told this story during one of my first classes at SWAS, and we decided to have a formal debate with Drake students on which program offered the best education. It was judged a tie by a local attorney and the school principal. Throughout the rest of my years in high school, I made several attempts to bridge the gap between the two schools, or at least to explain or defend the SWAS program. I ran for president of Drake - and lost. I became president of the SWAS Grievance Committee, the group before which any infractions of the SWAS school rules were brought - or more rarely, any complaints about a teacher or a grade. To think that I, of all people, would enjoy sitting on a committee that limited the freedom of my peers amazed me, but the experience instilled in me a sense of responsibility, especially considering how much under fire I felt SWAS to be. It made me realize how important it was that we not invite criticism of others through our behavior.

Finally, Martha nominated me for Advanced Placement English, taught on the main campus. One day the teacher made what I considered a very nasty comment about SWAS students, and I spent the rest of the period glaring at him. After class, I told him that since SWAS was having to work hard at dispelling such impressions about itself, it made it that much worse to have teachers add fuel to the fire. He treated me very respectfully, and suggested that maybe I should develop my sense of humor. In typical seventeen-year-old fashion, I retorted that a sense of humor was not the issue when people's well-being was at stake because of such talk. He agreed and never did it in class again. I have to give him credit for considering the feelings of a loudmouth teenager.

SWAS made me feel special and important. I imagine that my experiences at Drake had made me decide that I could no longer reveal my uniqueness. It was much easier to be unique in an environment in which you felt safe. At Drake, no one knew me or cared, and in fact it felt as if most were repelled by my attempts at individuality. Even if I kept quiet about my political views, kids would knock the hats I wore off of my head. I no longer wanted to stand out in a crowd; I needed to belong to one. SWAS was exactly that - a crowd of unique people.

It seemed to me that SWAS *stood* for tolerance. I thrived there. The students were people I wanted to be friends with, and the students actually liked the teachers who made me feel like learning again. My experience at Drake had made me entertain the notion that I was somebody who didn't need school - that I was intelligent enough to learn on my own and, if the traditional school was all that there was, that I was prepared to do it alone. SWAS teachers made me feel that learning in the school environment was fun and challenging.

I guess, to me, Drake was a microcosm of the larger community from which I felt expatriated, and SWAS was where the expatriates went. Without SWAS, I don't know where I would be today. I most certainly would have been a high school drop-out, and I don't know if I would have recovered from that or not.

I remember that after a couple of weeks at SWAS, my mom ran into Martha at the store. She came home and told me that Martha had said, "I love your daughter." Most recently, my teachers had had nothing to say about me - except that I was a pain in the neck. I can't tell you how good it felt to have a teacher say that I was loved. Loved. Shortly after that, I talked to Keith about problems I was having at home and he referred me to a family counselor. We only went once and our problems continued, but it felt extremely important to me to feel cared for.

Actually, all SWAS teachers made me feel that way. Basically, the teachers were SWAS. Of course, we might not have realized that then, but the teachers were probably in a very precarious position as leaders of this program; in charge of situations that could have gotten out of hand if not supervised properly. They nevertheless maintained approachable, non-dictatorial personas. I don't know how they did it. It was a fine line to walk, and they must have had an incredible amount of endurance. I was really pleased at the reunion when, during the slide show, made possible by all results of all of Rudy's photography classes, everyone burst into applause each time a picture of a teacher was shown. I hope that the teachers understood the applause to be our way of saying "Thank you."

I was also amazed at the acceptance SWAS kids had for one another; they were kind to those who were handicapped in some way or who exhibited less that normal behavior. I imagine the teachers had a lot to do with that as well, but unless I am romanticizing the situation, it seems to me that we went out of our way to involve students who were different or shunned at other schools. Friends I made in SWAS I still have. SWAS was a haven for students of all types, many of whom - like me - would have been disruptive in the regular program or, at the least, unproductive. There is a place for schools like SWAS in our society. Given what adolescents have to deal with, providing a school like SWAS is a profitable investment in those students who march to the tune of a different drummer.

Juli Gicker graduated from SWAS with highest honors, intent on studying law. She works now as a Presbyterian minister in North Carolina.

CHAPTER FIVE

SCHEDULING AND EVALUATIONS

Although any attempt to describe the evaluation process
makes it clear how incredibly complicated it was,
there can be no doubt that our constant evaluation
of students, teachers, and program gave SWAS real vitality.

A T THE END OF the second year, a thorough review of scheduling indicated several things. The indefinite time length for courses, some lasting only a week or two and others continuing all semester, was problematic. The teachers felt the need to establish consistent criteria for variable credit; haggling for credit vs. grades was clearly not acceptable to anyone. These two considerations, plus the recognition that both students and teachers functioned better with a clearer sense of the school's basic structure, led to the idea of breaking the semester into "blocks." For several years thereafter, we had five three-week blocks each semester, with the successful completion of each block giving one credit in that subject. It was possible then for some students to double up and receive many more than five credits in a subject each semester, and it was also possible for some to fall behind.

Another change was the institution of "tribes." Students were assigned to one teacher (randomly at first and then according to student choice) who served as an academic and personal counselor. Those two words - blocks and tribes - were to shape the structure of the school for the years to come.

Courses were scheduled for three weeks at a time, with the option of continuing if the subject warranted the extension. Geometry and French, for example, would continue year round, while students had the option of choosing from a wide menu of different classes to fulfill their English or Social Studies requirements. There were other advantages as well; attendance improved and students and teachers evaluated the courses and individual student progress on a regular basis.

There were several implications inherent in this system. Teachers had to craft new schedules every three weeks, a process that took several hours after school. New schedules were then printed and distributed. Five times during the course of each semester, students chose anew what they would study. Freshmen and seniors might end up in the same classes for English, Art, PE, Science and Social Studies - and even for math and foreign language at times. It is probably easy to imagine the difficulties here, but the benefits were enormous as well. Several staff members argued energetically that having mixed classes, freshmen through seniors, was going to be one of our school's true strengths. The fact that we were devising new courses each three weeks in every subject matter was challenging, but again the rewards seemed enormous. The curriculum was a living, breathing entity, something that students cared about as deeply as the teachers did.

Everyone in SWAS had the same Drake counselor who came to us at the beginning of each semester to sign students up for their official "course card" classes: English 1, World History, Algebra, Biology, Art and PE, for a typical freshman, for example. These were the courses that were required for graduation from the Tam District, plus electives. The staff then crafted choices within each course: perhaps "Whales and Dolphins," "Ecology Action" and "Animals Without Backbones" for Biology, to give one example. The "Ecology Action" seminar might continue for the whole semester, with different students coming and going, while "Animals Without Backbones" might just be offered for a single three-week block. Students were able to choose no fewer than five and no more than eight classes. A typical schedule might look like this:

Official Course Title	Mini-course	Time
English 3 (5 units)	Steinbeck (1 unit)	MWF 8:30
French 3 (5 units)	French (on-going)	MWF 9:30
Girls' PE (5 units)	Volleyball (1 unit)	MWF 11:30
	Tap Dancing (1 unit)	T Th 2:00
Geometry (5 units)	Graphing Formulas (1 unit)	MWF 1:00
World History (5 units)	The Middle East (1 unit)	T Th 10:30
	Child Care (on-location)	T Th 8:30
	Tribe Meetings (no credit)	T Th 1:00

This student would have free time (or unscheduled time as we preferred to call it) every Monday, Wednesday and Friday from 10:30 to 11:30, and would not arrive on-campus on Tuesdays and Thursdays until 10:30, after working at a local childcare facility. This was the schedule of a very self-motivated young woman, who took more classes than she needed and was willing to volunteer working with young children for no pay and no school credit.

It must be admitted that equally typical was the schedule that allowed a student to sleep in every day until 10:00 or leave each Tuesday and Thursday after lunch. Actually, it would be more accurate to say that they had no *classes* after lunch for many, many students found "hanging out" at SWAS to be the best part of the program. We often had to chase students home for dinner. It was also possible to take "Improvisation" for English and "Current Events Discussion" for History, for example, and have a far less rigorous workload than those who had chosen "Shakespeare" and "The Constitution." There is no denying how quickly some students figured this out.

The freedom of a loose schedule was difficult for some students to handle. Normal progress toward graduation was one credit per block in each course card subject. Some people made more, some less. If students earned more than five credits, they were "banked" until the following semester. Lost credits were easily made up, but the staff had to be vigilant to see that each student was taking the best advantage of the program. Here is a sentence from the "SWAS History Book," a document written as a one-block English class in the fifth year of the program. "There are two ways to take advantage of the SWAS program: the good way and the bad way. The good way would be using your free time wisely for both classes and on-location work or independent study. The bad way would be not taking challenging classes, hating every minute of school, just plain sloughing off. SWAS is flexible."

Some students took one course at the main Drake campus. Chemistry was not offered at SWAS as we had no lab facilities, and there were no Advanced Placement courses, so those students wanting them took a first period class at Drake.

Although any attempt to describe the evaluation process for classes makes it clear how incredibly complicated it was, there can be no doubt that our constant evaluation of students, teachers, and program gave SWAS real vitality. Student evaluations involved a great deal of shuffling of "Block Slips." Half sheets of paper were passed out on the first day of each block and students filled them in, one for each class they chose to take. The sorting of Block Slips showed us class size for each mini-course. Small boxes at the top of each slip allowed teachers to mark attendance and tardies, and a signed statement reinforced the students' commitment to the class. This portion of the form was the "Contract Slip."

At the end of the block, teachers wrote a paragraph about each student's work and awarded credit, but not grades, for the work completed. Students responded with comments of their own, often explaining, complaining or expressing pride in their progress. This portion of the form became the "Evaluation Report." Slips were collected and shuffled again according to the "tribe," and the teachers in charge reviewed each of his/her members' progress by sorting and reading through them all. In this way, students who had failed to meet expectations or who were not making progress toward graduation could be identified and counseled by the tribe leader.

Tribe leaders, then, took on most of the responsibility traditionally assigned to guidance counselors, overseeing each tribe member's schedule, credits and progress toward graduation. We did a pretty good job, but it was not unheard of for a senior to discover in May that she needed two more units of P.E. or a semester of fine arts in order to graduate on time. Some scrambling was often necessary. On the other hand, it was not unusual for a freshman to complete two years of English or science, depending on her interests.

SWASies' transcripts were a mess for the first few years: three units of English 2 and four of English 3 earned in one semester, for example. We drove the Drake administration and the counselors crazy, I am sure. Soon, we came to see that the sanity of the counseling office and the opinion of colleges and universities reviewing these transcripts were probably more important than our stubborn insistence on showing partial credit exactly as it was earned. We started to "neaten up" the transcripts and to assign credit in traditional units of five, often then carrying over units until the next year when a students might have several units "banked." Again, SWAS had a certain vocabulary of its own: "I have three units of Algebra banked from last year, so I just need two more this year, and my tribe leader and I agree that I should double up and start Geometry now so that after the first two blocks I won't be behind."

Completing block slips was not the only opportunity for reflection. At the end of each semester, students and teachers wrote extensive cumulative evaluations. After reviewing all of their block slips in each subject, students wrote one to two page evaluations of their work in each subject area. Teachers responded in kind. It seems certain testimony to our youth and enthusiasm as teachers that we were willing and able to write as many as 200 evaluations at the close of each semester - no checklists, no fill-in the blanks, but instead individual full-page narrative reports.

The final step for students, and one we emphasized so successfully that the term was always spoken with reverence and a certain sense of awe, was to write an "Overall Evaluation." These were often four pages long, combining introspection with detailed plans for the future, as well as providing, at times, a forum for explaining failures or complaining about teachers. Writing them was good therapy, I am confident. The "Overalls" were read by the tribe leader who then wrote a full-page personal response. When I contacted former students about the writing of this book, many told me they had kept all of the Overall Evaluations, written some twenty-five years earlier.

Next, evaluation conferences (ten minutes for each subject matter area and a half an hour for each Overall) were scheduled for each student. During Evaluation Week, each student would typically have six or seven subject matter evaluations conferences, and one long Overall conference, possible only when all the others had been completed. Tribe leaders would counsel each student about credits that needed to be made up, discuss how much effort they had put into their work and into the evaluation process itself, and guide them into reflection about future goals. However, I can also remember discussing everything from suicide to cocaine use, from divorce to nutrition in Overall conferences. The relationships between students and their tribe leaders were incredibly important, potentially powerful, and always deeply personal.

Teachers, too, were evaluated every year. Each of the other staff member and five students wrote evaluations for the teacher, who then wrote a self-evaluation as well. The depth and honesty of your self-evaluation was considered very important. Nothing I have ever experienced in my 40 years of teaching has ever come close to this process.

The entire concept of evaluations and the reflection they necessitated became the core of the SWAS program. It must be admitted, however, that when the school first opened, evaluation was viewed as a one-time event, a necessary hurdle to pass if SWAS were to be considered for inclusion in the regular Drake program. We wrote the first SWAS evaluation to convince the Board that we were doing what we had promised to do. This evaluation was made in connection with an independent assessment firm, and was framed with no thought of continuing the process after the initial two-year experimental period. We were trying to show that our program was successful. It was a single, albeit very high mountain that we had to scale only once before we could travel on level terrain.

Or so we thought at the time. Quickly, we saw the shortcomings of this model and realized the value of continuing assessment and evaluation as an integral part of the program. The word "assessment" comes from the French "to sit beside" and that captures the spirit of what we tried to do. Teachers and students sat, metaphorically and often quite literally, side by side and looked at how we were doing. We turned our evaluation process inward, evaluating ourselves - students, teachers, classes, program - over and over, simply in order to do the best we could.

CHAPTER SIX

SWAS FINDS ITS STRIDE: MEEGAN OCHS

SWAS is where I learned that learning is a goal, not a grade.
Doing well in class no longer meant getting an A;
it meant learning the most I could.

I WENT TO SWAS BECAUSE I had just moved to San Anselmo and my best friend Rachel was about to start attending an alternative school; I decided to apply there simply to be in school with her. I had always been a successful student, but not necessarily because I learned all I could from my teachers. When teachers did not seem to care, or did not see me as an individual, I still found a way to get an A that did not involve much work. When I got to SWAS, I felt empowered as a student for the first time. I was encouraged to find ways to received credit for extra curricular activities. I was a teen "rap leader" at Planned Parenthood and received elective credit for my training and work there. I also worked long hours on dance and drama productions, for which I received no credit at all.

SWAS was where I learned that learning is a goal, not a grade. Doing well in class no longer meant getting an A; it meant learning as much as I could. I never attended college after graduating from SWAS, but every time there has been a topic of interest to me, I have gotten a book and studied the subject thoroughly. This is the most direct influence that my years at SWAS have had on me. While I do not belittle the educational system, I know many friends who went to college directly after high school with no direction in mind, continuing their high school mentality and receiving little more than a diploma and a boyfriend or a girlfriend. I think you should go to school to study something that inspires you, and do so whether or not it prepares you for a job.

Now that I have a step-daughter headed off to college to study Musical Theater, I find the statement above challenged by the knowledge that she wants to be an artist, and the tremendous expense of education these days. I fear the debt she will incur, despite tremendous financial support from her family, could hinder her artistic efforts after school. We need to find a way for young people to continue their education, without crippling themselves with unending debt.

The importance of SWAS having its students involved with decision-making cannot be stressed enough. The Grievance Committee made decisions about disputes between students and teachers, and among students - important decisions. In addition, being involved in evaluating your own progress and participation in academic classes was amazingly empowering. I would have felt terrible giving myself a grade I did not feel I had earned. A third way that students were involved in making decisions was that we decided on our own projects and earned our own money for the projects' trips. Many of our parents were not well off. Not having to ask them for money, or worse not being able to go on a trip because our parents could not afford it, would have been very upsetting. This way, earning our own way, made us feel strong and involved.

I started writing seriously in a journal for the first time in SWAS. While there have been lapses, I have written consistently throughout most of my life. Once I had a child, I started writing to him a birthday letter each year, capturing interesting moments, milestones, things he said and experiences that I am confident would have been lost to time if not captured each year. I consider these journals and letters to my son my most cherished possessions, and the habit of self-expression and self-evaluation comes directly from SWAS. What I am writing to my son likely won't be of interest to him until he is a father himself, but what I gift I have ready for him because of how I was inspired to document these experiences at SWAS. I have also kept all of my evaluations and papers from SWAS. How interesting it is to read not only what my teachers thought of me, but also what I thought of my teachers, my surroundings and my class performance.

Another important element of SWAS was multi-age education. The students spanned grades 9 through 12, but we were not segregated by grade level. Some things were done in a multi-age group defined in the beginning of the year as our "tribe." Second semester classes were project based, and we worked together in classes designed to support the project we were doing together. I remember only two teachers from my first two years of high school, before I came to SWAS, and mere glimpses of what I learned there. The second two years, when I attended SWAS, I remember everything, as evidenced by the chapter in this book. Project based learning connected me much more deeply with everything I studied, in large part because it was in context.

I enjoyed all of the teachers at SWAS. I certainly had my confrontations with Chris, my math teacher and tribe leader, but that is inevitable with two strong personalities. She was a good teacher; I was stubborn and confrontational. I know I would get more out of her classes now. Our art teacher Max was always a joy. He let me do independent projects in art that encouraged me to make many beautiful things I still see at family members' homes. Eliene had very creative ideas for our English classes which lent themselves to the project each group was doing for the semester; for example, while reading *Dandelion Wine*, we did a play reading with a senior citizens' group, in preparation for seeing Edward Albee's *Seascape*, a play about aging that we would see in Ashland Oregon as part of our project. Rudy was the first person who made science fun for me. I had no interest in biology or chemistry, the traditional high school fare, but was fascinated by the courses he taught in astronomy and geology. His photography class, where we learned and practiced every step of the darkroom process, was a creative outlet for many of us.

It was Keith, however, who allowed me my most important independent study project. After working with Planned Parenthood, I became a birth control educator in school. I did get a few interesting calls from parents who didn't seem to be aware how lucky they were not to be grandparents. History had always been a favorite subject of mine. Studying about apartheid in South Africa before seeing *Siswi Bansi* at the Ashland Festival changed my life. Keith encouraged us to talk to local businesses that supported South Africa, such as Barclay's Bank, and confront them on the effects of their policies. This real life experience was very exciting for a high school class, and the bank, by the way, stopped its support of the South African government. We were powerful!

Last there was Martha. I felt the most personal relationship with Martha who was young, yet very maternal. I took English, French and dance classes from her, and it was she who read and commented on all of my journals. However, the most important experience we shared was working together on the Winter Performance. Helping to organize this performance was the culminating focal point of my years at SWAS. It seemed that everyone at the school was involved in some way. It was a true collaboration of the community. Talented students created dance routines, wrote original music, and performed scenes from beloved plays and movies. Martha led it all, and choreographed for the performance as well, but the students were empowered to work on their individual pieces. While I do not claim that I was the best organizer at the time, it is interesting that my career since leaving high school has been a combination of organizing the lives of individual performers and organizing large events. I have been the personal assistant to an actor, and have studied acting myself, landing small parts in several wonderful films. In addition, I raise money for environmental, human rights and social justice groups, organizing educational forums and fund raising events. SWAS gave me the confidence that I could make a difference, and taught me the skills that have made it possible.

My child attends the Open Classroom in Lagunitas, which is where many of the students who attended SWAS had their primary education. In fact, he has been in school with many children of my fellow students at SWAS! Martha volunteers in this school, so she was able to teach poetry to the children of many of her students. I know it was very special for me that my teacher was now teaching my child, and I feel confident others felt the same way. I've become very involved in the school, having joined the school board when my son was in second grade. Looking at what goes into running a school, especially an alternative school, makes me even more impressed with the teachers who devoted themselves to

SWAS. All teachers are unsung heroes, but those committed to alternative education face additional challenges. Discovering how to balance state standards with ensuring a vibrant education with engaged students is a tall order. I am even more grateful for the efforts of my teachers now that I understand more of the challenges they faced, and how gracefully they executed their task.

I am impressed with how many lifelong relationships started at SWAS. There are actually high school sweethearts who married and now have grown children. There are countless friendships that started there, and continue many decades later. Sadly, I have attended the funerals of several SWAS students, and now Rudy's and Keith's as well. As an example, Eben Twombly was a tremendous presence as a student at SWAS. He died very young, and seeing so many of our friends from SWAS at his memorial was powerful. Seeing all of our surviving teachers there was even more moving. This kind of connection cannot be commonplace.

Meegan Ochs Potter has worked for many years for the ACLU, and is currently a member of her local school board in San Geronimo.

CHAPTER SEVEN

COURSE OFFERINGS

*Yet it somehow never occurred to me at the time—the teachers
not only put up with it but seemed to enjoy it. The tap dancing,
the hammering, the constant painting, the tree-climbing:
they didn't just put up with it, it seems they
encouraged and delighted in it.
They believed our energy and enthusiasm
were essential to our learning.*

BECAUSE OF THE EVER-CHANGING Block schedule, I have a collection of schedules from over our fourteen years, most handwritten, a few typed, all with at least one spelling error or typo, run off on the mimeograph machine to be distributed to students. The staff met and proposed classes, students added their input either in person or through their tribe leaders, and then came the hard part: figuring out what to offer when so as to avoid conflicts. I can recall the board in Rudy's room covered with crossed out attempts to achieve the perfect balance. Then one of us had the job of copying the schedule and the course description for duplication, a task I secretly enjoyed.

Some courses, such as math and French, had a traditional form. Students could be enrolled in all of the math and French courses offered in the regular Drake program. Classes met regularly and were supplemented by individual tutorials. In math, students who chose to study the traditional mathematics topics, such as algebra and geometry, used unit study guides designed by the district math departments. They worked on basic skills at their own rate, moving from group to group as they progressed. In addition, special interests of students generated other math seminars or individual projects. For example, there might be classes in surveying, Fibonacci series or computer programming. On the other hand, there was also the opportunity to have calculus classes that met at Chris's house with a small group of dedicated students in what resembled a college seminar more than a high school class.

For French the format was also fairly traditional. Class size ranged from six students to fifteen, however, allowing an ideal informal setting for learning a language. The content was similar, if not identical, to that of the Drake program, in terms of the study of grammatical structures and vocabulary, but course work also included outside-of-class activities such as dining in a French restaurant, going to museums and seeing French films. After the first year, we did not have a teacher qualified to teach Spanish, but anyone interested in that – or Latin or chemistry, or Advanced Placement classes – could take classes at the main school.

English, science and social studies were courses that allowed for more freedom of choice, for both teachers and students. While math and French classes were naturally segregated by grade level for the most part, these courses had freshmen, sophomores, juniors and seniors all in the same classes. Biology students, for example, chose from block classes such as Audubon Canyon Workshop, Genetics, Dolphins and Whales, Anatomy, Nuclear Power seminar and Gardening and Botany. We took full advantage of our location near the ocean to focus on marine biology and oceanography. Duxbury Reef, the San Francisco Bay Model, Limantour Spit, China Camp Salt Marsh and Chimney Rock on Point Reyes were all sites for field trips and study. Physics students had field trips to Lawrence Radiation Laboratory, the Stanford Linear Accelerator and the UC Electron Microscope Laboratory.

Student choice dictated many of the social studies offerings, most of which stressed active involvement in the community. There were courses offered in Political Action, Justice in America, Utopian Communities, the History of San Francisco. Other, slightly more traditional – or at least schoolroom-based - courses were Ancient Man, the Constitution, Sociology, Economics and Current Events. The following chapter is an account by a SWAS student of one of the social studies projects.

English classes ran the gambit as well. One schedule that I have saved lists these courses: Weird Stories, Satire, Poetry, Black Literature, Children's Literature, Travel Writing, Lord of the Rings and "I Hate English," always a popular class focused on mastering the basics of grammar and writing skills. Once we started shaping our schedule around multi-discipline projects in the fourth year, it was easy to create English classes to deepen students' knowledge and understanding. Then we find English classes such as Hopi Mythology for the Southwest Native American Project, Shakespeare for the Ashland Project, Steinbeck for the Monterey Bay Project, or Argument and Persuasion for the Political Action Project.

P.E. activities ranged from the ubiquitous volleyball games, to tree climbing and bike riding. Ken Genetti recalled that bike riding in Marin County in the early 70's was a new and exciting venture. "This where the Mountain Bike was born. We were a little on the young side compared to Otis Guy, Joe Breeze and Gary Fisher, but the seeds of it were there! Riding on the mountain was totally happening by 1971 or 72. This was a very rich time to be a young person in Marin County associated with bicycles. It wasn't just that we were going to get on our own little bikes and ride to school. We were up in those hills. We were riding to Mill Valley, riding to San Francisco, regularly. This was a serious form of exercise and transportation and recreation. And I remember the klunkers we would build; those were the pre-mountain bikes, the one-speeds."

Ken remembered one specific adventure: "Richard Miller and I decided to take our bikes to the top of Red Hill, likely in the spring of 1974. He was riding a one-speed 'klunker' and I a three-speed Schwinn Traveler. We often made this arduous hike up to the top of Red Hill because it had such an amazing view. You could see down Ross Valley on one side and up Drake Boulevard toward SWAS on the other. Since there was o road up Red Hill other than the remains of an old switchback, the only way to get the bikes up was to drag them up the ultra-steep slopes. Was certain at the time that no bicycle had ever made it to the top and I would wager that despite the Mountain Bike craze that started in San Anselmo, no one has accomplished the feat since."

Another aspect of the SWAS program that many students remember fondly was the opportunity to teach classes themselves – not just extra credit classes, but "real" classes that were given grades and official school credit. "The SWAS students were allowed to teach certain classes: auto mechanics, haiku, yoga, SWAS Cafe, roller skating, volley ball, etc. SWAS students earned the same units/credits as did students at Drake, with exactly the same standards for earning those units. SWAS *was* Drake! That is the best part of being a School *Within* a School! I have Sir Francis Drake report cards, transcript and diploma," reflected one SWASie.

Another remembers it this way: "The energetic and magnetic Kathleen was a fellow student and a teacher as well. She taught tap dancing with such creative energy: in her class we were as likely to riff to reggae as to show tunes. It doesn't surprise me that with all her dynamism she's gone on to be a highly successful publicist. I contacted her for help publicizing a project recently, and reminded her of the fun we had in her class. She replied, 'Yes, we sure had a blast rocking Devonshire Hall in our tap shoes, didn't we? I can't believe the teachers put up with all that!' Yet it somehow never occurred to me at the time—the teachers not only put up with it, but seemed to enjoy it. The tap dancing, the hammering, the constant painting, the tree-climbing: they didn't just put up with it, it seems they encouraged and delighted in it. They believed our energy and enthusiasm were essential to our learning."

Because SWAS students wrote their own self-evaluations at the end of each block for every class, and then wrote extensive Overall Evaluations for each subject area at the end of the semester, there was a continued focus on careful reflection and clarity of written expression. I have had former students tell me that having the opportunity - in fact, the requirement - to evaluate their own work was the single most important aspect of their education at SWAS.

CHAPTER EIGHT

REACHING TO THE COMMUNITY: LAUREL HEADLEY

from a newspaper article written in her junior year

Newspapers praised our work and were amazed that students alone ran the video equipment, moderated the debate, and ran the entire event smoothly. There was absolutely no apathy among students that day.

ONE OF THE MAIN goals at SWAS is to learn how to become actively involved in the growth of the community around us. Our Political Action Project was created to do just that, and to add relevance to the courses we were required to take. The project began in September and ended after the November elections. It included our English, Social Studies and Math courses. The SWAS schedule was flexible enough so that we could spend a large part of our time in fieldwork. Within a week of our first meeting, we found ourselves spending evenings, weekends and almost all of our spare time in various campaigns for the election. We learned how to structure our time to make good use of free time.

The Social Studies class was usually used for organizing and coordinating fieldwork and for speakers and discussions of the issues. The English class met three times a week and we wrote (and rewrote!) many letters and articles for newspapers, kept journals of our experiences and edited tapes of candidates' speeches. When the math class in Statistics first met, the students decided that after leaning how to use statistical information that we would take an opinion poll to predict local election results on

Proposition 17 about saving the Stanislaus River, and a contentious Water Board race between conversationalists and developers. After studying the different types of polls possible for us to use, we decided on a "random stratified" poll, phoning 400 voters. The names were taken randomly from precinct lists, but represented the correct percentage of each party in the precinct. Besides learning a lot from the twelve questions we asked, we picked the winner of the Water Board seat and our results on Proposition 17 were very close to those obtained from a broader polling professionally conducted and published in the San Francisco Chronicle.

By far our most ambitious project was hosting a debate at school between Betty Florrey, Republican candidate for the Marin Municipal Water Board, and Richard Boylan, her Democratic opponent. The candidates themselves gave us credit for gaining far greater attention at this local election. Newspapers praised our work and were amazed that students alone ran the video equipment, moderated the debate, and ran the entire event smoothly. There was absolutely no apathy among students that day. The candidates seemed to be a little nervous since this was their first debate. We knew we had a real debate when they got into a mild disagreement. It was the first of many debates between Florrey and Boylan, and when the election results started to pile up a conservationists' win, we could only think what might have happened if we hadn't thrown the first ball.

Another issue that interested our class was the Warm Springs Dam in Sonoma County, just north of us. Students from SWAS visited three high schools in Sonoma and found that their opinions were quite at odds with those of the local residents. "I tried to talk to them and almost got stoned out of the class. I do feel we did a good job getting our views expressed. They were looking for a nice recreational lake and there was nothing we could say [about the environmental impact] to them," one student explained. They were pleased, however, that they left to a round of applause from one classroom.

Another group ventured further afield, going to Los Angeles tom educate voters about Proposition 17 with a "Save the River" group. They pounded the pavement, rang door bells, stood at shopping centers for hours and answered questions from confused voters. We plastered the area with "Yes on 17" posters and generally made a lot of noise. "We had good and not so good experiences which involved losing someone on the Sunset strip at 1:00 in the morning, hugging helpful policemen and listening to a strange woman tell one of us to start wearing a bra!" was the way one student summed it up.

During all of these endeavors we kept journals about our campaigning experiences. We walked also door-to-door and distributed pamphlets. We interviewed candidates and political workers, including Barbara Boxer who was then the field representative for John Burton. Many SWASies were disappointed by Proposition 17's defeat and angered by what we saw as the opposition's misleading advertising.

Laurel Headley is a lawyer in Berkeley, California, with a broad-based practice, ranging from complex federal white-collar and environmental crimes to state court misdemeanor and juvenile delinquency proceedings.

CHAPTER NINE

TRIBES AND PROJECTS

We renewed our commitment to the "Never everyone" motto,
but sometimes needed to be reminded of it, again
and again, at every turn along the way. No one idea
was good enough to force every student into.

I F THE FIRST SUBSTANTIVE change in SWAS was from an open Question-Centered curriculum to a structure based on Blocks and facilitated by tribe leaders, the second and probably most important change was to curriculum based around projects. In 2016, small learning communities and project-based learning have become accepted, admired and widely instituted. In 1980, there were no such terms.

There is no aspect of SWAS that seems more dated - and more embarrassingly politically incorrect - than the choice of the term "tribes" to describe the groups into which we divided the students (or more accurately, into which they divided themselves). Tribes were part homeroom, part counseling group and part curriculum-development centers. Our schedules changed every year, sometimes giving as much as two full days a week for tribes to develop their own course of study, and sometimes only having tribes meet briefly once or twice a week as a check-in for student progress in classes. However often or long tribes met, they nonetheless formed one of the strongest identities for students, Students would announce, "I am in Rudy's tribe" or "Chris's tribe is going snow camping" or even "My tribe is a bunch of losers." If teachers were honest, they had to admit that who was in their tribe, a year-long commitment, could make or break their entire experience of teaching. Teaching math or French or English was one thing; teachers expected to face a wide range of abilities and varying degrees of interest within any class, and could deal with that with relative ease. A great tribe, however, meant a great year; a whining, unproductive tribe meant misery for everyone. We all experienced both.

Teachers were called "tribe leaders" and we engaged in "tribal warfare," with competitions based on anything from the result of volleyball tournaments to attendance or grade averages. This warfare was quite positive, accomplished with a healthy dose of self-mockery, but the winning tribe was awarded with something quite real and very valued: a dinner prepared and served by the staff and first choice of class selection.

Although tribes were encouraged to choose names, they were usually just referred to by the teachers' names. Within each tribe, however, two names were chosen for each half-tribe or "Support Group." A bit more creativity came out here. Nikes and Adidas, Magic and Mystery, 2B and Not 2B were examples of Support Group names. Each Support Group met once a week for discussion or what at the time was called a "rap group." We enlisted an adult volunteer for each tribe so that each group could be kept to about twelve students. Support groups meetings were the best and the worst of SWAS.

They were the best when they became genuine support for students with problems. One student's mother simply left her, leaving a note and a twenty-dollar bill on the table of the home where she worked as a live-in housekeeper. The student was therefore on her own and with no place to live. The Support Group provided the avenue for her to find not only a place to live and a job, but also sympathetic ears. They were the worst when students and teachers both felt we were wasting time and just rehashing old complaints.

Projects grew out of these times of failure with tribes, or out of our frustration with them. During the third year of SWAS, we decided that tribes should meet two full days a week, and should work together to design a project to study in depth. The trouble was that since the tribes had been chosen by the students merely through their preference of tribe leader, there was little common interest that truly bound them together. It was next to impossible to sustain the interest of twenty-five students for a semester, even in an agreed upon project they had chosen themselves. Some of the ideas were novel and should have been great: an exploration of Fibonacci Series in nature and art or an extended study of the ecology of Bolinas Lagoon. Soon, however, there was rebellion in the ranks and interest dwindled. Also, both students and teachers tended to give tribe activities second priority, placing class days and required subjects first.

Therefore, we decided we would design the project first and then have students sign up for whatever most appealed to them. We renewed our commitment to the "Never everyone!" motto, but sometimes needed to be reminded of it, again and again, at every turn along the way. No one idea was good enough to force every student into. Students could choose the project that interested them the most or choose none at all. While some students doubtlessly chose projects in the same way they had chosen tribes, by selecting the teacher with whom they most wanted to work, they nonetheless made more of a commitment to the activities and preparations agreed upon by joining a project. Rock climbing and camping became a popular focus for many students.

Warren Fairbanks, our first art teacher, remembers how the transition from Blocks to Projects came about for him and for the students who chose a different focus: "The major event during my period there was the January block. That was a dream come true. For one month there were no bells, no other commitments except the many magnifications of ART. We attended numerous museums and galleries throughout the Bay Area. In addition, being regulars at the San Rafael dump, we scrounged for materials we intuitively felt had the potential to merge within themselves to be so much more when creatively united. An unplanned bonus was that during the process we too became united; sharing all of our discoveries and accomplishments allowed us to forge a special bond. The whole experience was a distinct joy of learning (it really can happen!).

"As I recall, the Environments (large and often elaborate structures designed to create personal spaces within the art room) were a spinoff from the January block. We knew where to get our art materials and we knew their value. Minimal money was used. A couple of bucks could acquire some material at the dump. The workers there had a section where items thought to have monetary value were placed separately, and we came to know it well. There was also a great economic lesson presented by the dump in as much as they made money three ways: first, they charged people to discard unwanted material, then sold some items and materials, and, after compacting the rest with heavy equipment, sold or leased the property. English and Social Studies lessons emerged as well as we immersed ourselves in this extended project.

"Treasure Beach on the Mendocino coast was another resource depot. An old abandoned dump had, through time, deposited broken glass pieces, completely smoothed by the perpetual waves, on to the beach. 'Out of mud grows the lotus' ... another lesson." This non-conventional approach to art meant a great deal to many students. Ken Genetti remembers, "The environments were also little structures. You think about these people now in Tokyo who have these micro-apartments, and that's kind of what this was like. We had the urge to make a shelter, our own little space. The art program at SWAS was one of the most liberating and exciting things that I participated in. Warren Fairbanks, the art teacher, was this amazing guy who let us do just about whatever we wanted."

Yes, too, some students still saw projects as another name for a field trip - and usually an extended one - but again there was buy-in to the classes leading to the trip. Students could earn required credit from classes while preparing for a project, while others, not involved in the project, could still take part in the classes. In the first year, for example, there was the Wilderness Project and the Ashland Project, two that repeated successfully year after year. Students in the Wilderness Project studied the geology of the Sierras, the history and writings of John Muir, while learning compass skills and rock climbing techniques.

Those in the Ashland Project read the five plays to be shown at the Ashland Shakespeare Festival, and studied the history of the periods portrayed. Math skills were used in planning expenses and money raising projects. People skills were essential in planning menus and clean-up routines. There is no way to overstate the importance of this last aspect of every project trip. We camped out - no hotels, no restaurants. If a group of five students was responsible for making the dinner on the first night, and then left dirty dishes for the next morning's breakfast group, there was definitely something to discuss. On a more serious level, if a student brought marijuana on a project trip, the repercussions for him, for the teacher in charge, and for the whole group were something that needed to be addressed immediately. We learned a lot.

We developed what came to be called the LSD Rule (a title that seems embarrassingly cavalier to me now). It stood for "Liquor, Sex and Drugs" - the three things not allowed on any school trips. Students were required to sign a contract, stating that they understood and would abide by this rule. The punishment for breaking the LSD Rule was severe, the most severe of any in the history of the program. First, the offending students would be sent home by bus at their parents' expense, and second, they would be out of the program the next semester. Because this consequence was seen as so severe and was so dreaded, it acted as a good deterrent.

One student who lived with a single mother with far less income than most Marin County residents has explained to me how important it was to her that students going on a project trip were simply not allowed to pay for it themselves or have their parents pay. The fully accepted routine was for the group as a whole to raise money. For this student, this allowed her not only to participate in projects that she could not otherwise have afforded, but also allowed her the dignity of being on the same level as her more affluent classmates. Car washes, raffles, and bake sales raised hundreds of dollars.

Projects provided some of the most memorable moments for staff, as well as for students. Chris remembers the Pioneer Project, where we determined to live like pioneers--only wool blankets, tarp, basic staples for food. The group made a trial run before the trip to Sierra, deciding to spend one night in Point Reyes. "We were going to make candles for light, but when the rains poured down, we huddled under the tarp trying to cook and make candles. It was miserable ...so in the early evening we bailed. On the real trip to Bishop, we were hunkered down with our wool blankets--lesson learned, make sure the blanket is long enough to cover your feet. I remember the place was infested with rattlesnakes. I was terrified, but trying to be cool. I found a little 'island' in the creek to toss my blanket. Then several students decided to kill and cook a rattlesnake. Yikes--it was wiggling in the pan and I couldn't stand it. 'Tastes like chicken,' they said as they chowed down." It was a trip to remember.

I went on the second Pioneer trip, this time on horseback. We hired a guide, but still got so lost that we had to make our way on horseback down a nearly vertical cliff. My head was almost touching the rump of the horse. Like Chris, I somehow mastered the art of pretending not to be terrified. Our dinner and campsite was authentic alright, but I worried about the "authentic" diseases we might be taking back with us, after drinking from the small creek.

The Wilderness Projects probably provided the most hair-raising adventures. On one trip, the group split, with one teacher going off one direction, and a second in another. Days later when they reunited, only to learn that one young student, Scott, had gotten lost and a bear had gotten most of their food while they were out looking for him. He turned up the next day, thrilled to have found his way back to the group. The great part was that Scott had remembered to do all the things the teachers had taught: get out of wet clothes, get into sleeping bag and stay warm, stay still and don't wander around. Once he was found, I think he felt like a conquering hero, surviving a night alone in the wilderness."

Chris again: "How about the other wilderness trip to Emigrant Wilderness? Again, I had gone a different direction with one student to get the cars. Rudy and Dave went with the kids. I remember sitting and watching them straggle across Kennedy Meadow and mentally ticking off who was coming along. Everyone was in except for one student. Where was he? I had followed him for days in the woods and had told Rudy to keep him right in front of him the remaining time, 'never out of sight,' because I'd seen how unaware this particular student could be about his surroundings. Rudy said he'd been right ahead of him as they came down the trail into the meadow; we fanned out and searched. The streams were raging and I was terrified. Finally, I got a rental horse and headed up the trail. About then, here comes the lost child, with a big smile, wandering out of the woods., completely unconcerned. He had somehow managed to get off the trail, which was really like a freeway in this area. I was furious, but really just so relieved that he was OK." All in all, we were incredibly lucky never to have had a serious accident or to have actually lost anyone.

CHAPTER TEN

LOOKING BACK: MARTIN SIRK

In writing this piece, I asked myself "How did my SWAS experience shape my life?" My strong interests in science, nature, and outdoor activities were all initiated while in high school; attending college only strengthened and formalized them.

I ENTERED SWAS IN THE fall of 1975 as a freshman and remained in the program until I graduated four years later. These were the program's middle years so I did not experience the early growing pains, nor the sadness of its closing. In grammar school, I was always a smart kid, but never a great student; most of the time I was just bored. My decision to attend SWAS did not stem from any desire to save the world (or myself), but primarily based upon a visit by two student recruiters who came to my junior high school, and a on a conversation with a neighborhood friend who had just graduated. What they told me about the program seemed vastly more interesting than what I had experienced in school so far. I told my parents about it, and fortunately, they agreed.

Two aspects of the SWAS philosophy strike me as significant with thirty years of hindsight. The first is that the majority of classes were integrated with respect to age. Any class (except math and foreign language) could be populated by kids from any grade level. Once you got to know a few folks from other grades, they became your friends rather than objects to be feared or tormented. The second important feature of SWAS is its interactive approach to learning where students discuss ideas and solve problems with each other (both in, and outside of class) as opposed to the traditional teaching format of lecture followed by relevant homework. As a science teacher today, I embrace the interactive approach. Although unaware of it at the time, my teaching style was certainly influenced by my SWAS experience, both as a student, and as a student teacher.

Most accounts of the SWAS program that I have heard emphasize the projects. Yes, they were great fun and good PR for recruiting purposes, but I also feel that they genuinely provided unique learning experiences that allowed the SWAS philosophy to become fully manifest. I participated in projects every year; the diversity of which still amazes me all these years later. The first one occurred in the fall of 1975 and centered on our country's bicentennial. Eileen Bundy, with the help from Larry and Art, two UMass student teachers, led a dozen students on an ambitious four-week journey across the country (by car!). We visited numerous historical sights and cites relevant to the founding of the United States. The entire trip cost us $200 each which we earned beforehand doing bake sales, car washes etc. We mostly camped, but also stayed a friends' houses, churches, and on one memorable night in Memphis, at the Salvation Army shelter. I still remember sleeping in the bunkhouse with several drunks and eating a wretched breakfast of leathery eggs (I still hate them). Eileen's knowledge, drive, and determination made this trip possible. I feel lucky that an adult would take a bunch of teenagers on a one-month field trip. As the youngest member, it was intimidating at first, but the older students quickly adopted me and remained my friends for many years afterwards.

1976 was an election year. Jimmy Carter came out of nowhere and clinched the Democratic Party's nomination for President. Keith Lester put together a group of classes focused on politics. In one class, we went to a Democratic Party rally in San Francisco and watched a televised debate between Carter and Gerald Ford. In this same election, Barbara Boxer was running for Marin County Supervisor against June Weeden. We sponsored a debate between the two candidates at Drake High School. I was the time-keeper and distinctly remember telling Ms. Boxer her time was up on a particular question! We also precinct-walked for her. This involved first canvassing our assigned neighborhood to find Boxer supporters, then calling them up on election night and remind them to please vote. She won, and I have been following her career ever since.

In my junior year, Chris Anderson, with her husband Dave, led a group of us to climb Mt Rainier in Washington. To prepare our selves we engaged in a variety of activities including long hikes, rock climbing, map and compass navigation, and an all-night hike out in Point Reyes. On the giant volcano itself we were in heavy clouds day after day. We eventually gave up our summit bid and started down the mountain on a partly clear morning. Soon, however, we found ourselves in a white-out where snow and cloud are indistinguishable shades of gray. Off to one side someone noticed a dark mass. "What's That?" A giant yawning crevasse! We had wandered off the safe ridge route and onto a glacier. Without hesitation Chris yelled "Rope up!" After we were all tied in and spread out, we discussed what to do next. Miraculously, the clouds parted southward just long enough to take a compass sighting on a lake. Combining this single reading with our altimeter, we determined we were about a half mile too far east. We decided to head back up the mountain the way we came for a while (since we knew there were no crevasses in that direction), then continue west. I was roped in thirty feet behind Chris and my job was to bark out orders to ensure that the line between us was pointing in the right compass direction. After a couple hours or so of anxious slogging, we came across a trail wand.

We were back on course, and Chris and I were heroes.

Each year I took a course down on the main campus, so I had an idea of what regular high school classes were like. To my Drake peers, however, I was just one of those SWAS hippies who hung from trees and smoked out on the back steps. There was no provision for the regular students to take part in SWAS activities, so they never had a chance to witness our program from the inside, nor appreciate its attributes.

In writing this piece, I asked myself "How did my SWAS experience shape my life?" My strong interests in science, nature, and outdoor activities were all initiated while in high school; attending college only strengthened and formalized them. I can't think of a single college course, experience, or activity that altered my path significantly. This fact surprises me, and illustrates the power and importance of a good high school education during this formative period of life. I am lucky to have been immersed into such a great high school environment, and to have had teachers who really cared.

Martin Sirk works at Lawrence Livermore Laboratory in Livermore, California with a specialty in astronomy.

CHAPTER ELEVEN

THE STAFF

True, if the term "dysfunctional" had been
around then, we might have applied
it to our family at times, but we were a
family that never stopped reaching
for ways to become more functional, more open and more supportive.

S WAS WAS A PRODUCT of its time, true, a time when "educating the whole person" was not yet a cliché, but it became more than that. The current academies and small learning communities now so eagerly embraced and so conscientiously researched in universities today are echoes of this same concern, this same commitment. The one difference, as Jackie Moskowitz has noted, was that our program truly came from the interests of students and a small group of teachers; it was "bottom-up" educational reform in a way that more recent attempts at reform have not been.

SWAS came into being in troubled times. I suppose the same could be said of almost any period of educational history, and certainly of today, but we faced a population of very bright, very sensitive students who did not accept the status quo and who were eager both to be seen as unique individuals and to be part of a supportive group, a family if you will.

The image of SWAS as a family is so pat, that it is easy to dismiss it, but throughout our years together, that is the term that best describes the school. We were a family. True, if the term "dysfunctional" had been around then, we might have applied it to our family at times, but we were a family that never stopped reaching for ways to become more functional, more open and more supportive.

It worked. We provided more of a family than many of our students had had before - in their homes and certainly in their school -- and more than some of them have found since. The voices at the reunion told us that; the calls we get from students twenty five years after they graduated tell us that; the postings on my Facebook page when I reached out to former SWASies tell us that; the stories in this book tell us that.

Part of the reason any family is successful is the strong relationship between the parents. The SWAS parents were the staff. There were five and sometimes six teachers working at SWAS at a time, but four of us were there consistently. Chris and Martha, Rudy and Keith became the parents. Our personalities, and our different weaknesses and strengths combined so that we seemed to cover every aspect of parenting. As in any good marriage, we learned a great deal from one another. We spent more time together than we spent with our spouses; with the structured "sharing" time we scheduled for Wednesday afternoons, we probably sometimes communicated better with one another than we did at home.

We took risks, got angry, laughed and supported one another. I remember one SWAS spouse coming home after work to find the whole staff gathered in his living room, listening with complete attention to one of us talk and cry about the death of a child. He sat at the edge of the group and just listened. I remember realizing that he was in awe of the openness and the closeness within this group, and also that he probably felt a little left out.

He wasn't the only one. The solid four-sided configuration of Chris-Martha-Rudy-Keith was so stable that the fifth teacher often felt left out, often was left out. Without intending to, we formed a unit that was hard to penetrate. We worked so well together and had such a long history of understanding the nuances of each others' communication that although the changing parade of fifth teachers always brought enormous resources and talents, they probably never felt completely at home.

Chris was the natural leader of our group. She later became assistant superintendent of the Tam district, where her serious demeanor, sharp intellect, and absolute, unwavering clarity about expectations made new teachers tremble in her presence. It always amused me - and I assume her - that she was seen as such a rigid, authoritarian figure; she was "the man," the establishment to many who did not know her well. Anyone who had the privilege of working with her, either in the early days of SWAS or as a district administrator, knew that her ideas were progressive, her heart warm, and that the welfare of students was always her first priority. Chris taught me a great deal about organization, and also gave me the confidence that I, too, was an organized person and a potential leader. In the beginning, she may have had more confidence in me than I had in myself. She was our department head for so long that it was hard to think of anyone else filling that role, but when she went on leave, she convinced me that I could fill that role. I did.

She also taught me to say no. I remember one simple incident that somehow made a lasting impression on me. Chris and her husband owned a large van (what would be called a SUV today) that we called Big Blue Bertha. Bertha was often used on SWAS field trips, and I asked Chris one day if I might use Bertha to take my students in the Twentieth Century Art class to a local museum. She said, "No." That was all, just one word. I was taken aback, hurt and more than a little paranoid. What had I done? Why didn't she trust me? My mind started to run wild. It wasn't more than one minute later, however, that I realized there was a perfectly clear explanation (which I have now forgotten) about why the van had to be someplace else at that time, but in that one minute the proverbial light bulb went off in my mind. A person could say no. *I* could say no. I am not sure that I am describing this well, but it is a moment that has stayed with me for decades.

There were other lessons as well. Chris could confront students and peers with directness and without rancor, when she felt they had done something wrong. Chris spoke her mind. Chris never lost sight of our goals and worked to find ways to meet them, without letting herself be sidetracked by "cool" ideas that were only distractions. These were strengths I did not possess. If Chris was our head, I was seen the heart, the soft touch, the emotional one. I remember that heart metaphor used in many of my evaluations, but in truth I probably did not deserve that label.

If SWAS had a heart, it was Rudy. He taught us all about the everyday beauty and strength of love. He provided that so necessary sense of steady support and unconditional acceptance for the students and the program - I am tempted to say the heartbeat. Rudy and I taught a class together called "The Birds and the Bees," he providing the scientific knowledge and I, in theory, providing the humanistic backdrop necessary for open discussion about sexuality. It was an amazing class. After a few class meetings where the basic plumbing was discussed, most of our class time centered on the topic of relationships, trust, fears and, perhaps surprisingly, death. Rudy was the calm center of it all. Never have I met a man with such quiet dignity.

Keith, on the other hand, was rarely quiet. He combined a warm, outgoing personality with a gift for words. We taught students to be interested in politics, current events and ecology, and more importantly, he showed them how they could be actively involved in issues they cared deeply about. Never at a loss for words for ways to express his feelings, he was a marvel to me. It was he who taught me to get angry. He taught me loyalty. Keith and I took twenty-five students to the Southwest for three weeks. I do not think I could have survived that trip without him - or with anyone else. We were so very different, yet found ways to laugh at ourselves. I remember a group of students literally cheering when I finally stood up to him about some decision he was making for us all. It was another light bulb moment, for the world did not stop, I got my way, and we loved each other still.

It was really very simple - and very rare. We loved one another. The four of us supported one another, not only emotionally, but I want to say physically. It was as if our four temperaments formed four sides of a balanced structure. Our strengths complimented one another's. Lastly, we laughed together. In fact, maybe it was the long series of in-jokes we shared that was most off-putting to other teachers. Others teachers could have taught as well or better, and each of us has worked with other groups productively after SWAS, but never have we had a marriage quite like this one.

When SWAS disbanded - I am jumping ahead - I knew I would miss the time with the staff more than anything. To this day, we all realize how fortunate we were. I remember suggesting we could be like the early Christians, meeting secretly or even not meeting but knowing with a glance or a secret sign that we shared something special. This was presented as a light-hearted analogy, but there was something spiritual about what we shared. (Even as I write this, I can also see the raised eyebrows of half of the group over my choice of this word) It was something as simple as love. The early Christian analogy worked too; we often shared a glance across a crowded teachers' meeting and now, after more than thirty years, are able to connect immediately, even after months apart, about one another's hopes and struggles. These are the people who helped me develop into the teacher and the person I am today. I am very lucky to have had them in my life.

If Chris, Rudy, Keith and I were the solid core of the staff, there were other very important teachers as well. Warren Fairbanks and later Max Poppers taught art. Warren had the students construct "environments" in the large double room that served as the art room. He taught students - and me as well - that we are all artists. "Art is everywhere" was his mantra. I still have small "pocket museums" that he made for me, and more importantly, I have my own art pieces that he inspired me to create. Another one of Warren's sayings was "You may graduate in four years, but you take your body with you." An avid runner, he inspired many students to form lifelong fitness routines. If Warren brought a wonderfully humorous cynicism to the program, Max brought a cheerfulness and enthusiasm. His art room was colorful and busy, the handmade environments replaced by paintings and leatherwork.

Both Warren and Max encouraged students to decorate the building. One detail-oriented girl took a full year to paint black and white squares on the foyer ceiling and precise strips on the walls. Other students painted Grateful Dead logos on the walls and each individual locker became a canvas for expression. We were a colorful school. We even installed a large rainbow over the external door of the building.

SWAS had three other wonderful English teachers, Karen Emmons, Eliene Bundy and Kate Blickhahn. Karen was only there for the first year but left a lasting memory on all for her students. Eliene was our grandmother - but the sort of grandmother who marched in every peace march and protested most every rule. She was courageous; she was bold. Eliene took students on SWAS's most challenging and ambitious project trips. She and twenty students drove across the country to Washington D.C. One telling snapshot says a good deal about Eliene: when she announced it was her birthday, and that she was turning 55, one of our students sat back and pronounced with awe, "Whoa, maximum speed!"

Kate Blickhahn was also with the SWAS program for only a year, our last year, before becoming principal of Redwood High School. She had been instrumental in starting the Bay Area Writing Project and had a national reputation as an educator and leader. If we were not sure her quiet demeanor and very "respectable" ways would translate well in our somewhat rowdy program, we also knew that she would have a great deal to teach us. We were wrong to worry, and right that she had a great deal to offer. She used the year with us to pilot ideas she had not been able to incorporate in the regular school English curriculum. Her Medicine Wheel class, based on Hopi traditions, was both rigorous and innovative. She taught classes in Transcendentalism, and in Women's Literature. Both Eliene and Kate broke stereotypes about women in ways that were very important for our students.

There were others as well, Pat Lusk who came for one year, Ken Boeri for another. Carol Brady, a wonderful math teacher, was with us briefly as well. We also had an ever-changing parade of student teachers. The University of Massachusetts sent us several dozen over the years. These bright young men and women added a great deal to the program. I wonder how many of them have remained teachers and how they look back at our program.

My Creative Writing class in 1979 made a plan to have a reunion on the top of Mt. Tam on the first day of spring in the year 2000. We figured it would be a date we could all remember. At first, we thought it would just be for the students in this one class, but word spread. I did not know what to expect; this was four full years before Facebook. However, twenty-one years later, with no formal reminders, dozens of students and all the teachers showed up. By 2006 and 2010, Facebook and email connections meant that many more attended more formally planned reunions. As I write, I am hoping this book will be ready for the August 2016 reunion.

CHAPTER TWELVE

STAFF PERSPECTIVE: MARTHA ALLEN

*There is no doubt that the project trips provided
the most important teaching/learning experiences
- and not always in lessons we intended.*

I WAS ONCE AN AVID journal writer. Maybe that too was something that went with the times, for I have not kept up that habit and am sometimes embarrassed by the narcissism, masked as self-doubt, that I see in my old journals. Through them I have a record of what I considered the major events of my life during the period I taught in SWAS. Reading my journals, the chronology is clear to me; major events such as family deaths and births provide the first sign posts, yes, but what strikes me looking back is that I am reconstructing my life through SWAS projects. 1973? Death Valley. 1974? Anza Borega. 1976? First Ashland trip. 1981? *that* Ashland trip. Was my life so centered around this school that these project trips have provided my memory's most sturdy framework? For years, we bemoaned the fact the so many students tended to think of SWAS in terms of the "field trips" they could take, and yet here I am summarizing my adult life in much the same way.

Projects became an established part of the SWAS curriculum by the fourth year. There is no doubt that the project trips provided the most important teaching/learning experiences - and not always in lessons we intended.

I went on several project trips; the longest and most ambitious was the Southwest Native American Project (or SNAP) for which we had a full semester of preparation and then a three week trip to New Mexico and Arizona with twenty students and two teachers. (This was not *the most* ambitious project trip in SWAS's history as Keith drove students across the border to Baja, and Eliene escorted fifteen students across country, by car, to Washington D.C.,-- but she was always the bravest of the staff.) For the SNAP Project, students had history classes with Keith that focused on Native American history and the geography of the Southwest. Warren offered ceramics classes in which students studied and tried to replicate Hopi pottery and Navajo baskets. Rudy taught classes in desert ecology, and I had students reading Frank Waters' *The Man Who Killed the Deer* in one English class and Native American myths in another. Students were responsible for raising the money to go on the trip; we had car washes, raffles (probably as illegal then as they are today) and music concerts.

The lessons learned on the trip ranged from the mundane (who would cook and who would clean - and when) to the transcendent (hiking across Canyon de Chelly or exploring a Hopi village). We also had four flat tires and a near drowning. We had fights and love affairs. I hated it and I loved it; I will certainly never forget it. I think I can name almost every student on that trip that happened over thirty years ago.

The trip that will always stay with me, however, was externally far less challenging. I had taken students to the Ashland Shakespeare Festival for many years. We always read all the plays ahead of time, planned our camping and food preparation, and set out for the four hour drive for Emigrant Lake Camp Ground. At times we had snow in May or 95 degree weather in March, but the trip was usually uneventful. Students eager to see Shakespeare and Ibsen tended to be studious, well behaved and cooperative. In 1981, I went with a group of students I had come to feel especially close to. I *know* I can name all sixteen of them: Joyful, Robin, Sean, John, Kate, Chris, Geoff, Amii, Erin, Danielle, Annemarie, Andre, Matthew, Jodi, Eric and Dan.

It is difficult to find words for what happened on that trip without lapsing into cliché. The plays we saw were responsible for some of what happened; we saw a performance of *The Birthday Party* that was incredibly powerful and very depressing. That night, students stayed up talking most of the night. *Death of a Salesman* sparked more discussion. How different the play was for them on stage than it had been reading it from the page in the classroom! "Attention must be paid." Even *Twelfth Night* provided powerful grist for the mill. Malevolio was portrayed as a far more sympathetic character than our classroom rendition had made him. Lastly there was a play called *Artichoke* which I do not remember except I believe it had the line "I am an island of calm in a turbulent sea," which became our collective comic mantra.

Many students on this trip could be labeled as "troubled": a boy with an acute stutter, another who lived in a group home for mentally disturbed teens, a young woman who was openly gay, and many who came from families facing the ravages of divorce or drug addiction. In addition, one student had cerebral palsy and had to be carried up the stairs of the theater and looked after in intimate ways for which I was not prepared. As a group, they talked for hours about the death of parents, and their fears of going crazy. Something happened within that group, however, that I had never experienced before and have never since. I can find no word for it but love. I have had wonderful feelings of community and communion with groups of students and with friends, yes, but this was something else.

My journal tells of my worry about the well-being of some of these students - well-founded in many cases - and my anxiety about balancing on the line between authority figure and friend. The nightly discussions were difficult, but we laughed a lot as well. I remember cooking tacos in a downpour, playing my first and last game of "Dungeons and Dragons," and hiking around the lake to find wild flowers. I remember the boy with a stutter talking, with absolutely no trace of one, to the girl whose parents had just disowned her because she was a lesbian. I remember the way other students helped the boy from the group home overcome his acute anxiety by giving him simple half-hour tasks: Let's take a walk; Why don't you go do your laundry now; Come help me with dinner, etc.

I feel as if I saw miracles on that trip. The connections with those students lasted well beyond the trip. I made referrals for a few of them - for drug counseling or for therapy. I wrote letters of recommendation for others, praising their maturity and leadership abilities. I am still in contact with some of them today. That kind of connection simply cannot happen in a regular high school. Ashland 1981 defines SWAS for me.

CHAPTER THIRTEEN

THE STUDENTS

Many of us had been through the Open Classroom in the Valley,
and so our whole education was in alternative schools.
We were sort of an experiment, it seems to me.

I N MANY WAYS IT is hard to describe SWAS students, for if the program taught us anything, it taught us not to depend on stereotypes and not to generalize. In the beginning, we were seen as the hippy school. Externals supported that: hair, drug use, music preferences and a certain in-your-face attitude. Within the mix, however, there was enormous diversity. While it would have been difficult to find many who were politically conservative, there was a wide range of religious belief - or lack of same. Internal differences in assertiveness and self-confidence were evident. Students in those first years reported, almost without exception, that what they valued most at SWAS was the feeling of acceptance by their peers and the staff.

Soon enough, however, we were the punk school. The first Mohawks I had ever seen were sported by twin SWAS students. I remember walking into the girls' bathroom and seeing a student dying her bright pink hair jet black as she calmly announced to me, "My mom loves my hair. She said I could have it any color I wanted, as long as it wasn't black." In fact, the restrooms became the focus of much of SWAS's identity. The girls' restroom was painted with unicorns and fairies, while the boys' room had a mural which became an ever-changing canvas for political and social expression. A parent complained about the "graffiti" in the boys' restroom and the principal, Tom Lorch, had it removed, much to the dismay of the SWAS students. The memo he wrote to the staff shows an admirable balance of humor and leadership:

As of Monday morning, the graffiti in the SWAS boys' room will be painted over. R.I.P. It is being removed at the recommendation of a Board member, after the filing of a complaint. I hope that after a year and a half of that mural's glowing presence, its removal does not become an occasion for concern. I attempted to find and call you on Friday when this matter arose, but was unable to locate any of you.

One former SWASie put it this way, "I showed up at Sir Francis Drake High as a sophomore. I was the kind of kid that did not really fit in anywhere. There are at least two reasons for this: I switched schools a lot, never really establishing any long-term childhood relationships and I hung out with my older siblings a lot, therefore exposing me to all sorts of adult things. I was five of six in the family stew.

"What drew me to SWAS were the students. I was not fitting in at Sir Francis Drake High School, hiding behind a lot of curly hair and Vaurnet Sunglasses. On my second or third day at school, I saw, for the first time, a punk! I had never seen anyone like this in my life. Living in Lodi, California, from age nine to sixteen, I'd never seen any punk rockers, not at Lodi High yet anyway. I first witnessed a SWAS student from the main campus of Sir Francis Drake, a skinny boy who was often bullied and chased by main campus jock types. More than once, I had seen him running across campus with a couple of apes on his heels. So, of course, I followed him any time I saw him. Finally, I stumbled on to the back steps of SWAS. I had myself transferred there immediately, and just that quickly, befriended that skinny punk boy."

Another described the school culture: "I remember sitting on couches and calling my teachers by their first names. It was the first time I had felt so much respect from my teachers and felt empowered to direct my own high school experience. We were given freedom, sometimes surprisingly so, but also the creativity to come up with what we thought was valuable to our learning and growing and what classes we thought appropriate to get credit for.

"I do remember falling flat on my face, trying to teach a poetry class that I knew nothing about. I remember falling in love for the first time with a boy named Michael. He would bring me flowers and balloons as well as breakfast with decaf coffee from the cafeteria every morning. Mostly, I remember taking driver's ed class at the main school and impressing the teacher so much with how supportive we all were to each other. He said he'd never seen students treat each other with so much respect before in all his years of teaching driver's ed."

The freedom SWAS offered was used in different ways by different students. "It was a very loose time for teenagers. Every school I went to had an unofficial 'smoking area' designated somewhere on or very near campus. On the Drake main campus it was at the bleachers (Bleacher Creatures!) and at SWAS it was the back steps on Saunders Ave. The teachers at SWAS were concerned about my self-medicating behavior and spoke to me about it more than once, but that intervention works best from home. Thanks for trying guys! I think the purpose of SWAS for me, at that time, was to help me realize that I was not the only misfit. The students and teachers at SWAS made me feel liked and accepted."

Others used the freedom differently. "The first week I arrived in SWAS I decided that I wanted to graduate from high school in three years, and the program allowed me the flexibility to do that. I was able to take more classes, get some credit for college courses at night and get into college a year early, which was great. I just remember feeling comfortable, feeling that I was accepted, even if not understood, by my peers, and feeling that the teachers respected me as an almost grownup and trusted me to make the right decision (most of the time!), and that enabled me to become more independent and self-possessed."

In contrast, another student reminded me that she had taken the class called Gumption, in which we all decided on something we wanted to change, a resolution if you will. "I actually quit smoking because of it!" Several students over the years have told me that they stopped taking drugs because of a specific conversation they had had with me or other staff members. I remember driving two students to rehab, and one to the local mental health facility when I felt an intervention was necessary. Probably one of the most foolish things I did was to "hold" the cocaine paraphernalia of a student who asked me to help her quit. I am sure there were many others whose drug use I did not see or guess at. After the fact, one boy, now a successful businessman in New York City, told me of dropping acid on our yearly nine-mile runs at Bear Valley. I had no idea.

Others whom I contacted for their memories and reflections about SWAS spoke of being reluctant to mention drugs, for fear of giving the school a bad name - or probably for fear of upsetting me - but there is no doubt that drug use was prevalent among the young people at this time. Now as parents, these same students see things differently: "Now, 20 years later, I am a successful graphic designer, specializing in food packaging graphics. I have a teenage daughter who is happy and busy doing rowing and ballet. Am I a little over protective? Definitely!"

Still others thought back to the musical and artistic expression they had discovered at SWAS. I was struck with how many former students were still exploring music and art, professionally as well as as an advocation. "The music in SWAS was fantastic. The students were so creative, from the murals they created on the walls to the concerts, both in school and all over town. I was so proud of my boyfriend, the drummer. I was also so proud to be able to paint my own locker any way I wanted to." One girl created an intricate checkerboard pattern on the ceiling, a task that took her many months to complete, while others opted for a Grateful Dead logo or a simple flower painted on their lockers.

For many years, SWAS put on a Winter Performance. It started as a dance recital, with most of the pieces choreographed by me and a talented student teacher. Soon students were creating their own pieces, and we added musical numbers and comedy skits. It was never a fund raiser, but like our celebratory feasts, it provided many students with insights into what they wanted to do later in life.

Someone recently reminded me that SWAS students sometimes referred to themselves – fondly and proudly – as SWAS monkeys. I had forgotten that. It is true that we were sometimes seen as odd, outside the norm. In turn, it is clear to me that experiences outside of the classroom have often the most lasting impression. Kyle Thayer, now an architect in Marin, remembers, "It was the tree climbing, the art and the bikes that were really key. And I have to say, that the actual classroom work was … less special. Tree climbing became for a small group of SWAS students a real physical activity, a serious enterprise, not just an escape. There was a real physical component. I remember that sycamore tree, right there in front of SWAS, where there would be volleyball happening in the courtyard next to the auditorium. There would be volleyball and then that tree. Unlike many trees that we would climb, this was very public – almost like a symbol of something, right at the entrance to the school. It felt like people that weren't into climbing trees would see us and 'Oh, those are the guys who are climbing trees.' I loved that that tree was so public. You could share in a conversation taking place on the steps right below us.

"And it was at the top of this really tall tree, right next to the school, there was a nest. Part of the philosophy of the nest, unlike tree houses, which many people would have a memory of, was that there were no nails used, no metal hardware. The philosophy was that we were using Gilligan Island's technology – lashing twigs or wedging things into V-shaped slots in the tree, and making it kind of low-tech. That was part of the aesthetic of it, really. It was a construction technique. I look back at those nests being somehow related to the work I've done as an architect. There is a deep urge that people have to make shelters."

Another student remembered, "When I was applying to SWAS the guidance counselor at my middle school told me 'You don't want to go there, that's for troubled kids. You're smart,' and I told him, 'If you don't recommend me for this program, I will drop out of school and go work at Jack in the Box and it will be on your head,' so he backed down. I think I had scared the hell out of him. I had gone to an alternative elementary school and then was dropped into the middle of a traditional middle school amid everybody with their raging hormones and same haircuts and clothes. I felt like I freak. When I arrived at SWAS, which was filled with 'freaks,' I felt at home right away. People might still think I looked or acted strange, but they wouldn't shun me for it. I am still friends with folks from SWAS more than 30 years later. I also appreciated the critical thinking skills I learned there. Now when I run into adults who can't think critically, it shocks me. How can they not be able to parse a situation and analyze it properly? How can they swallow what somebody else told them without breaking it down?" This same student reminded me that she had spent her entire freshman year on roller skates, and "that that was okay. Down at the main campus I had to take them off, but up at SWAS, they never came off. Nobody cared." By sophomore year, she was on solid ground.

There was another subset within SWAS that made me smile, both at the time and now as I look back at it: The SWAS Motorcycle Club or SMC. It consisted of perhaps eight boys who talked tough and *some* of whom owned motorcycles. All, however, were interested in learning to fix motorcycles and cars, and the staff brought in student teachers to accommodate them. These boys did not fit the stereotype of the SWAS monkey as pictured by those on the main campus; they were clearly not hippies, nor punks, nor tree huggers, nor really non-conformists at all except within the SWAS community. Somehow they all fit.

Yet another current within the SWAS population is worth a closer look: students who were gay. While some felt the need to stay hidden, many individual students were quite forthcoming about their sexuality. It was usually the girls who came out to me, sometimes proudly and sometimes with a sense of shame. I am still in contact with many of these women now. There were certainly no LGBT support groups, but the school population was open and accepting. "My situation was shared by many at that time... bigger families, less parental supervision and steering ... no clue what to do if your kid might be gay, and my mom had two of us. My brother should have been a dancer and I should have been allowed to play hardball ... and wear something other than frilly little dresses. I am crying in all my childhood pictures because I am dressed like a girl."

Now, she added, "I have been with my partner for eight years. We are hoping to someday get married. We live with our two daughters, 13 and 12, in Marin County. My daughter will most likely attend Drake High School. I hope there are still places within high school for the misfits, as there will always be kids who do not feel as if they fit in with the typical crowds."

Another student wrote "Simply: SWAS is still with me every day. My best friend today (and for 25 years) is a SWAS graduate. My present girlfriend is a SWAS graduate, my younger brother attended SWAS until it closed. I feel lucky to have been part of a family whose relevance in my life carries through to the present moment. I was confused, angry, self-centered and already depressive in September of 1980 when I met with Chris and Keith and they told me I could start there immediately as a student. In other words, I was a fairly normal 15 year-old boy. Ten days of Drake had left me feeling isolated and I remember telling my parents that I was "boycotting school." A friend's parents were mutual friends with friends of my folks and news of SWAS came to our family that way, I think. Also, I was told that SWAS was 'cooler' than Drake. It's not a stretch to say that the social skills that SWAS gave me, through Tribe and Support Group helped save me as an adult. Within the term of my sophomore year, I had developed close, lifelong friendships. Martha, Keith, Rudy and Chris showed that they cared about us as people through their actions, and Martha and Chris in particular pushed me academically - something I wasn't used to and prepped me for a much more successful college career than I expected.

"My home life was chaotic during the early 1980's for several reasons and SWAS was a haven of unconditional love and consistent behavior on the part of the teachers. Thirty some years removed, I still have conversations all the time with people in my age group where they talk at length about how isolated, uninspiring and unsafe their high school experience was. They often talk about the 'scars' they carry from treatment by other students and teachers. It is in those moments that I feel a profound gratitude for the work put in by the SWAS staff. Creating a positive place for a kid to grow and thrive might be the best gift you can give this world and I'm thankful to Martha, Chris, Keith, Rudy and Eileen for that gift."

One last comment from another grad: "I think the kids at SWAS were much closer than those in the average high school. I'm still in touch with many and have spent time meeting their families. It's been a joy. Most people you speak to don't have much contact with high school friends as they grow up. But SWASies seem to have a special bond. I'll never forget the joke. How many SWASies does it take to change a lightbulb? Answer: Ten, one to change it and nine to figure out how to get credit for it."

CHAPTER FOURTEEN

IN MEMORY: EBEN TWOMBLY

*One woman for whom English was a second language
remembered her initial difficulty understanding what the phrase
"Let a smile be your umbrella" meant, only to understand it
fully once she came to know the protection and shelter of Eben's smile.*

EBEN TWOMBLY HAD AN enormous smile for everyone. He was an extrovert, a loyal friend and a natural leader, awarded the status of "Distinguished Citizen" by the staff the first year he came to SWAS. He was funny, bright, interested in math and the sciences and, above all, in the outdoors. He thought he might become a ranger.

This chapter was going to be written by Eben. He and I took a hike in the spring of 2011 and discussed this venture, one he was eager to contribute to. I had not seen him for twenty years, and was happy to hear about his wife and two children, and about his very successful business. He was undergoing treatment for colon cancer at the time, and although he was realistic about what he called the "statistics" of his disease, he was also optimistic and determined to fight it. His funeral was the following winter.

My clearest memory of Eben is of his standing at the base of "The Perch," a 50-foot tree whose top had been cut away to allow a small, wobbly platform to be attached. I scaled the rope ladder that hung from the platform with relative ease, but then the next task was to stand up on the platform and then leap to a trapeze just beyond reach. I had managed to sit on the platform, but that proved to be a bad decision, for there was no room to maneuver my feet under me and to transition from sitting to standing; I was stuck, physically and emotionally. Eben stood calmly at the foot of the tree, and talked me through the process of leaving the relative security of my seated position, going back down a few rungs of the ladder and then kneeling and ultimately standing on the tiny platform. The leap to the trapeze was the easy part! He must have stayed with me for 15 to 20 minutes, patiently and quietly urging me to take each step at a time. He seemed to be absolutely sure I could do this. I know I could not have done it without him.

Those same qualities were ones that each speaker at his funeral praised: his supportive nature, his optimism, his generosity. his love of nature. One friend spoke about Eben's love of rock climbing, an activity he learned from Chris and her husband Dave at SWAS; another spoke of the many camping trips he and his family had taken, the last one only a month before his death. Others told story after story of his, at times, wicked sense of humor, another quality we all knew well at SWAS. One woman for whom English was a second language remembered her initial difficulty understanding what the phrase "Let a smile be your umbrella" meant, only to understand it fully once she came to know the protection and shelter of Eben's smile. Anyone who knew him at SWAS would have agreed completely.

I came away from his funeral thinking about what a remarkable experience SWAS has been for teachers and students alike. What brought this home more than anything to me was not so much that Eben's life and values were so clearly shaped by experiences he had learned in our program, but rather that his funeral, 24 years after his graduation, was attended by four of his former high school teachers and many, many former high school classmates. Not many of us will have that experience.

During our walk last spring, Eben made an apology. He had been one of a small group of students who had brought marijuana to Ashland on one of our project trips. I had found out through an overheard conversation in the girls' bathroom that someone had brought drugs, had asked for - and gotten - a full confession from the those responsible, and had then collected and flushed the marijuana. A tough, but honest, group meeting followed, as did consequences for all who had smoked when we returned home. On the hike that spring, Eben apologized not so much for having brought the marijuana, although he acknowledged that what he had done was clearly against the law as well as our school's written policy, but rather for what he termed his "arrogance" afterwards in failing to understand how awkward and uncomfortable it must have made things for me, as the only teacher on the trip, having to deal with this. Not many of us will have that experience either - an opportunity to reflect on adolescent misbehavior and attitudes and then to apologize.

It has been a gift for me to meet SWAS students years later, to learn what they have done with their lives, and to hear what SWAS meant to them. Most lament their failure to find anything close to it for their own children. The words "family" and "community" are the ones I hear most often in these conversations. Eben's funeral felt like a family reunion of both the saddest and sweetest sort.

Another former student wrote me this: "New to Facebook, I found a few names of people I remembered from SWAS, but Eben's name was different enough that it was easy to find him, and tell him how much that his moment of genuine support, one he probably did not even remember, meant to me, even 30 years later. I sent him a message, telling him how fondly I remembered him and his kindness. Only moments after sending that email to Eben, I read the sad post about his passing, on the SWAS group page. I wasn't sure I had understood correctly, but feared the worst.

"Back in high school I was already living on my own, since I was 16, struggling to continue and complete my high school education. I had very little support, so my SWAS friends were my family. Eben knew little of my struggles. It was a sunny day, I remember, and many of us SWASies were outside in front of the SWAS building. I don't recall what exactly had upset me, but I remember feeling deserted by my own family and support network, and completely hopeless, and I was crying a bit. I hoped no one noticed my tears, and soon classes were starting, so everyone was headed inside. But Eben noticed that something was wrong, came over, and took a few minutes to sit with me, making himself late for class, so he could be supportive. We had many of the same friends, but we were not close. I remember his comforting plaid shirt clearly, as I soaked his shoulder. Meanwhile, Eben tried to tell me that everything was going to be alright.

"Eben was right, things did get better for me, and after that day, I considered him, one of my sweetest friends. Now, I teach my daughter that small genuine moments, given to people, do make a big difference, and are appreciated, and never - ever - forgotten. From a smile, and a caring look, to simply listening to a person in need, the world cannot have too much kindness. Eben lives on, in me, and my family."

Eben Twombley graduated from SWAS in 1981. After getting an engineering degree at Humboldt, he started his own business in green building and engineering.

CHAPTER FIFTEEN

STUDENT GOVERNMENT AND DISCIPLINE POLICY

Perhaps the most remarkable thing about SWAS was the ability of the program to teach at once the importance and value of community, while at the same time helping students gain the personal strength to be individuals.

THE CLOSEST THING TO a student government in SWAS was the General Meeting, held once a week in Keith's room. I have a strong visual memory, enhanced no doubt by memories of photographs taken, of the room crowded with almost one hundred students, sitting or lying on the rug and balanced on the window sills. The agenda was fluid, but discussion usually focused on ways to improve SWAS, and often arguments broke out about what had been said, decided or not decided in previous meetings. One specific topic that was the source of dissention was that faculty meetings were closed to students; rumor had it that the staff discussed who should be kicked out of the program for "mushing out."

By the third year, a more representative student government was developed called the Bored (sic) of Directors, with representatives from each tribe and an elected president, secretary and treasurer. Perhaps ironically, the topic of who was "mushing out" became the most common one here as well. Students felt that others who were sitting on the front steps or playing volleyball for hours at a time were giving the program a bad name. They were, of course, absolutely correct!

SWAS had always had open enrollment, with a waiting list based simply on the date of application to the program. Developing selection criteria was suggested and a Screening Committee, a group of twelve students and one teacher, took on the task of deciding who deserved to be in the program. This committee recommended that perhaps a handful of current SWAS students be interviewed about their reasons for being in SWAS - because of suspected vandalism and because they had been "hanging out in trees" - and only one student was actually asked to leave. Perhaps uneasy with having the authority to actually expel someone from the program - or unsure about the legality of that - we then organized the

Grievance Committee to take care of any complaints that a student or teacher might have. The complaints ranged from a student's not receiving the grade or number of credits he felt he deserved to a teacher's accusing a student of stealing photography equipment.

One specific problem - and its solution - comes to mind. SWAS had a small office with a desk, file cabinet and phone. Students were free to come and go here as they pleased. Our phone bill was the highest of any department in the school, and analysis showed it was simply the great number of local calls over the MaBell allotment that was the cause. Numerous solutions were suggested, ranging from hiring a full-time secretary to devising an elaborate spy system to monitor calls. Finally, a simple $1.35 lock was put on the phone and students made personal calls at the pay phone in front of the Little Theater.

Being a member of the Grievance Committee was seen as a true honor and responsibility. The entire school voted and the five students with the highest number of votes were elected. The staff also selected its representative. Because the Grievance Committee had final say in any dispute, they were sometimes referred to as the God Committee.

Another light-hearted yet very important recognition for students came in the form of the Zelda Awards. I do not remember what the awards themselves looked like - we probably traded off the task of hastily making something at the last minute - but at least twice a year, we had an impressive awards ceremony. Half camp, half sincere, these awards were highly coveted. Chris, with her deadpan delivery, was always the best at handing them out. There is a drawing of the SWAS "trophy," seen on the cover of the SWAS yearbook. I think it was a couple of flip-flop sandals, and a feather, painted gold. The trophy itself was ridiculous, but to win it was considered a true honor.

It was the very freedom given to the students at SWAS that made the prospect of losing it seem like a severe punishment. One former student remembered it this way: "At SWAS there were no bells, no hall passes, no detention, and we had an open campus. We were free to sit on couches, and put our feet up, recline in an overstuffed chair or in a tree to study, and be seated next to our friends, wherever we wished, even if it was on the floor or an open windowsill. SWASies addressed teachers and tribe leaders by their first names, and we had awesome lockers, painted, and decorated inside and out."

She continues, "As SWASies, we were held to a more personally involved level of responsibility, for our own education. For example, our own self-evaluations for each class were considered when our teachers decided on grades. All of these freedoms made us feel a sense of ownership and belonging to our school, and to one another. You did not want to lose that. Contrary to popular belief, SWAS was not a continuation school. Once admitted, you had earn the same amount of credit, as Drake students did. I believe that every semester, those SWASies who didn't make enough units were either sent back to Drake, or transferred to the continuation school, depending on their performances."

It was when the staff was forced to enforce the "LSD Rule" (no liquor, sex or drugs on field trips) that the reality of being "thrown out" of the program became clear. There were cases in which parents argued strongly that their children not be given this consequence, seen as *so* severe, "just because" they were found with marijuana. I remember when one parent, a lawyer, threatened me with a lawsuit for enforcing this rule; her daughter, my student, backed both me and my decision, much to her creditß I felt. Students who fell behind in credits were counseled to enroll at the main campus, but the LSD rule was the only thing that forced an expulsion from the SWAS program. Most who were asked to take a semester away from the program came back. "Once a SWASie, always a SWASie," one reflected.

The influence of the program has proved to be long lasting. Dov Hassan, a college professor, wrote this: "I had a great time being a student at SWAS. There is so much about SWAS that was positive, I really can't understand why there aren't a whole bunch of programs all over the country that follow its model. I think that people outside of SWAS viewed it as a loosely structured place for a lot of teenagers to just hang out. This was definitely not the case. SWAS had a complex structure that was designed by people who were truly interested in an education that helped develop the whole person. The teachers and students who designed SWAS did a brilliant job of mixing academics with developing social skills, while valuing the interests, perceptions and contributions of each individual. I give much thanks to those who went before me and did the hard work of creating the school I was fortunate to attend for four years.

"A key component was the teachers, of course. The group that defined the school for the whole of its existence were all caring, devoted teachers who were passionate about their subjects as well as being people who had genuine interest in their students as people. They guided the program, but also let the voice of the student body help shape the structure and content of the school.

"Perhaps the most remarkable thing about SWAS was the ability of the program to teach the importance and value of community, while at the same time helping students gain the personal strength to be individuals. In fact, the two concepts were thoroughly intertwined, and not taught through lecture but through activity - many, many activities, constantly emphasizing these two themes. A few examples: go back packing with a group, then take a solo overnight; meet in a class room for several weeks with other students and a teacher, then, at the end, write a self-evaluation of your own work for the semester and talk about it with the instructor; have certain courses which must be completed for graduation, but be given the option to choose your own courses from one semester to the next. And many times individuality was 'taught' by just leaving people alone, to be whoever they chose to be. These are just a few examples that stand out to me, but I think these concepts were core to the SWAS experience.

"Another part of SWAS I loved was the appreciation for silliness and irreverence. I think these are underrated human traits, and students and teachers at SWAS seemed to always find a way to make this a part of any activity, whether it was the Winter Performance or some sports competition or a holiday celebration.

"I also want to say how my experiences at SWAS affect my approach my own teaching work today. I teach theater arts at a Bay Area junior college. Although I've been a student in many acting classes over the years, I find that when I am teaching beginning acting classes I rely as heavily on my SWAS experiences as what I learned in graduate school. To my mind, the first thing a student in an acting class needs to be able to do is take risks. And at the start of the semester, many of my students, being 18-20 and never having acted or gone to SWAS, the risk of simply standing in front of a group of strangers is huge. So my first job is to make them all be not strangers anymore. In other words, I spend considerable time turning the group (often 35-40 students) in to a sort of community. As part of my classes I use various games, some of which I learned while a student at SWAS, and set ups for interaction, that lead people to finding commonality and acceptance in each other."

CHAPTER SIXTEEN

THE LAST YEARS: JAMES GRAHAM

So inspired, I taught a class called The Novel Project;
interested students needed an outline and the first two or three
chapters of a book that could possibly see the light of day.

I FIRST STARTED "HANGING OUT" over at SWAS sometime in 1981, when I had made the acquaintance of some SWAS students. I felt welcome at SWAS. I felt as if I were being encouraged to join. At the time, however, I felt so unsure of myself and everything I was doing that I couldn't make the move. A year and a half later, there was a small voice in my head that was gaining some volume, and it said to me, "You are at a crossroads: Do you want to be 'normal' for the rest of your life, or do you want to make your own path and figure out who you really are, to be on the road less traveled?" Once I heard that, and realized that I was going to have a hard time with it whether I was part of the mainstream or not, I figured I might as well jump out of my box while I still had the chance. Any small fears were quickly allayed by the warmth with which I was received by the teachers, my peers and younger students alike.

I knew Rudy, vaguely, from my childhood, as my older brother, Tony, was a friend of his son, and I knew of Martha only by virtue of her marriage to my middle school art teacher. I immediately liked the block schedule, where different classes happened on different days. This gave a huge amount of flexibility; I discovered that getting two days of homework done over a day and a half is actually easier than getting one day of homework done overnight. Not having anything immediately due the next day gave my mind a chance to stretch and assimilate what I had learned.

Being able to call teachers by their first name was a very interesting concept. I didn't feel like these people were teaching from a podium or that they were clad in some opulent fashion, talking down to us. They spoke to us, and with us, and they shared their wisdom in a very subtle way. Learning became something to look forward to, a joy, and the friendly, easy manner with which we related to the teachers made it so much simpler to really ask for help. By the same token, we could just engage in casual conversation about anything under the sun. Martha, Chris, Keith and Rudy were all just downright fun to sit down with and talk to. There were no questions left unanswered for those who could bring themselves to ask them. SWAS was a boon for those present in mind, those aware and awake enough to ask the questions.

The students could, if they wanted, come up with a concept for a class that they wished to teach to others. I had always wanted to have a creative writing project with higher ambitions, one that would invite the students to come up with a story that they would turn into a book someday, not simply the essays or short stories that most conventional English classes required. So inspired, I taught a class called The Novel Project; interested students needed an outline and the first two or three chapters of a book that could possibly see the light of day. I learned some very important things about teaching:

* Sometimes you end up not teaching that which you intended to teach.
* It is very easy to honestly critique the works of people whom you have come to know. Grading appropriately said works is very hard if you do not feel that you have a firm ground on which to stand
* Teaching is nowhere as easy as it looks, and it actually doesn't even look easy in the least.

One of the best things about SWAS was the project trips, and the involvement in planning them. No one was ever turned away for lack of money; in fact, it was a requirement that the group earn money rather than depending on the largess of families. This meant that all students were on equal ground, and it meant that the planning and fundraising efforts were enormously complex. I wish I could have taken away with me some of these organizational skills, because while I really enjoyed the voyages we took, I can never seem to make them happen these days, children notwithstanding.

Two stand out in my mind, in particular: the Ropes Course, and the Vision Quest. There wasn't so much to prepare for in the Ropes Course. One went, and pitted their ability against the equipment and because of the safety factor involved, it was very easy to just relax and enjoy oneself as one explored the fringes of their limitations, and built them up to be stronger. The Vision Quest, however, was a multi-course event. We prepared for a three-day solo in the wilderness. There was a VQ English course (for which I think I still have my notes), there was a VQ core course where we learned both the philosophy and basic survival strategies necessary. It seemed that all of the teachers were involved at some point. We learned the importance of weaning oneself off bad foods before the trip so that the fasting would not be so hard on the body; we prepared to open our souls to the wilderness, to be open to everything that was going to happen, to let the Earth and the Air and the whole Universe read us as open books, and to write its lessons in the margins and the blank pages therein. I expected a lot from the Vision Quest. What I expected, of course, was not what I got, but the subtleties I did learn have been with me since, all through my life. Although I didn't get what I expected, in many different ways I got more than I expected.

In late April or early May 1983, I was punched in the gut by dread: The school district wanted to terminate the SWAS program. Wait - *my* SWAS program? The place that had served more than any other to truly stimulate my imagination, to open the straight-and-narrow box I'd lived in for the past twelve years, to really show me what the world could be when people work together? I was not about to idly sit by and let this happen. I sat and wrote out a thoughtful essay regarding the benefits of SWAS to students, what it gave, and what it provided, and how it truly encouraged especially those with some social difficulties to come out and not be so afraid to share their ideas. I don't recall if I got to read what I'd written to the Board of Education, but I know that I gave it to them. There was a lot of support at the school board meeting that night, and there was much discussion. It seemed to have an effect, because the school board elected not to close SWAS down, or so that was what we heard. I thought SWAS was safe.

I got the "two" of the "one-two" to the gut when we all gathered in Keith's room soon afterwards, and Rudy announced that the teachers had convened and agreed that SWAS would be closed, and my last year there was SWAS's last year. How does one react to that? After having gone to bat to keep SWAS going, even though I was graduating, and then to be shown that SWAS was going to fold in and close anyway?

I cried. I mourned for the path that was no longer going to be open to the classmen to come after me - all the opportunities that they would not have under the guidance of a union of wise and wonderful teachers. I grieved that those like me - socially repressed, inept to a point - those who most needed this kind of school were going to be turned back to an environment in which they would again be ridiculed, harassed, misunderstood. This wasn't fair to them, and it was very hard to accept the decision. But there it was. The staff had decided, and stuck to their guns, and that's something that deserved respect, in spite of anything else I felt. I don't think I was angry about it for very long, but I was definitely sad for quite some time.

Everyone deserves a chance. SWAS gave a lot of people that chance, myself included, and for that, I am very grateful. There are days that you may think, "I will never forget this feeling." Poppycock. You will forget. You will make up things that happened that didn't, and you will forget things that did. Mostly. This doesn't mean you can't be reminded, I have found. Of late, I happened upon a photo or two taken of the 1983-84 SWAS graduating class gathered in Samuel P. Taylor, some of us with our mortarboard caps, sitting, talking, looking over at someone who is speaking. And everything about that day came flooding back to me - playing frisbee, talking with everyone, receiving my SWAS diploma (which I still have and should probably frame at some point; the signatures have faded), as well as the passive senses of that day: the smell of the warm air, the feel of the sunshine down on me, and just the buzz in the air about us.

There was a twinge of sadness knowing that we weren't coming back, that we might not see the people around us for a long time, that we might not see some of them ever again. We were all somewhat learned, and all still somewhat innocent, embracing the world with open arms or running headlong into it, and looking back on the journey we had taken. This is a day that, at various points in my life, I will remember. I wish I could go back and feel that way again. I wish I could go back to a world that wasn't so frightening as the one in which we live has become. I am grateful to consider the teachers from SWAS among my friends. I am grateful for the opportunities that they gave me. These are things I will definitely not forget.

James Graham graduated from SWAS in its last year, as a member of the class of 1984. He now works in computer technology.

CHAPTER SEVENTEEN

CLOSING OUR DOORS

Ropes Course? Bear Valley Run? Do I have to go?
Do I get credit for this General Meeting, this tribe meeting?
What do you mean, we should plan a feast for the whole school? Why?

TOWARD THE END OF our thirteen years, we had become so good at saving "lost sheep" that the balance we had been able to maintain within the student population began to be lost. We had always attracted the non-joiners - the hippies, the punks, the computer nerds, the avid ecologists - but among the students who might inspire those labels were students of varied abilities and motivation. We had strong leaders sincerely determined to find the best education they could for themselves. Now, SWAS was beginning to be seen as a continuation school or as a place for those who could not make it in the main school. While the last years saw many strong, self-motivated students and true leaders, it also brought more who found the SWAS program a good place to avoid hard work.

As chaotic as the first years were when staff and students worked together to craft the sort of school they wanted, at least there was active involvement and genuine caring about what the school would develop into. Students now entered, accepting the program as a given, and complaining about activities that previous students had seen as vital parts of the school. Ropes Course? Bear Valley Run? Do I *have* to go? Do I get *credit* for this General Meeting, this tribe meeting? What do you mean, we should plan a feast for the whole school? Why?

Times had changed as well. Colleges and universities were losing patience for the unorthodox and often confusing transcripts that SWAS students left with. Eighteen credits of English sophomore year and only two in junior year? Why do you have so many Independent Credit units? What did you *do*? The mid-eighties looked different from the early seventies. In many ways, it was just that simple.

There is also no doubt that the teachers were weary. Thirteen years is a long time to maintain the energy and commitment necessary to run an alternative school. Chris put it this way, "I think the changing student clientele was the most important element in making the decision to close - there were just not enough high energy, positive role models and we were tired of providing all the spark. Our spark was dimming too."

For staff and teachers alike, it sometimes took the passage of years and the wisdom of hindsight for us to truly appreciate what an amazing place SWAS was. Kathleen Fatooh put it this way: "It really only came home to me, how truly special that SWAS program was, a couple of decades later when I had children of my own approaching school age. We found an alternative cooperative pre-school and had a fun year there, and then we had to face the big decision."

"Back in childhood," she continued, "my closest-aged sister had blazed trails for me. When she took dance and then horseback riding lessons, those possibilities, which I might never otherwise have thought open, presented themselves to me. When my sister went to SWAS, I knew that was where I wanted to be when I reached high school. And when we were grown and she had children a few years older than mine, I saw their delight in homeschooling and thought that might be what I'd do with my children, too.

"But, true SWASie, I didn't make the decision for my children. I sought out parent information and we visited the closest schools and schools that were cited in the district for excellence, magnet schools and charter schools. We saw programs with mixed-age classrooms and curriculum that was intended to be child-led, and my children actually attended here and there to try it out, but those were short-lived experiments. "My children wanted to have what I had had a taste of in SWAS: the opportunity to choose to study what interested them, not 'put away your math books now because it's time for history.' No matter what their philosophy, the schools we tried taught herds, not children. Teachers full of enthusiasm were forced to teach to standardized tests, and the mere placing of 20+ kids in a room with one adult meant that a huge amount of time was spent on crowd control, very frustrating for the children who were interested in what was being taught and those who were not, alike! I observed that when children are forced to study and aren't engaged, the result is mayhem that must constantly be controlled.

"The home school motto, 'The World Is Our Classroom,' was a comfortable fit for me from the first, probably because of SWAS. Our home school learning loosely patterned itself after SWAS cluster projects. If a child was interested in trains, we researched trains and learned about their mechanics and their effects on society. We visited train museums, rode trains, talked about trains. When a child became fascinated by fish we spent hours observing wild fish in shallow ponds doing a mating dance, helped maintain fish habitats, visited fish stores and public aquaria, and the child (6 to 8 years old during the Fish Years) read, studied statistics, wrote and published articles, and corresponded with experts about fish. Learning was interdisciplinary and fun, not because I was a great teacher, but because I gave the children the right to lead, saw myself as a facilitator rather than a pundit, and drew on experts in the community. There were lots of books out at the time about homeschooling for excellence and my sister Carolyn was steeped in theory and passed along literature, but I think I really first learned how to teach when I learned to learn at SWAS. The goal of our home schooling was to learn how to learn, and learning was driven by curiosity."

Kathleen continued, "There was one area that concerned me, starting out as a homeschooler. It happened to be an area where there had been some failure in my high school experience: record keeping. It was the responsibility of a guidance counselor, who worked for the main high school but counseled SWASies, to tell us how we were doing credit-wise and make sure we had all the classes we needed, to graduate. Many of us were told at some point in the final days of our senior year that we lacked enough credits for graduation. In my case this turned out to be an error in his records; in some cases friends had to attend summer school unexpectedly.

"As for college prep, I never heard of the SAT tests until I overheard classmates talking about them. I was terrified: 'What, we need to take a test to graduate? Oh, to go to college? Why didn't anyone tell me!' I don't know if the teachers were aware of how poorly we students were served by the counselor, and I am sure they didn't know that I for one had parents who were completely disconnected from involvement in my academic progress and plans. I don't know where the whole problem stemmed from - probably a combination of factors - but it left me throughout my college career ever-vigilant of requirements and watchful for test dates. I ended up with an MFA from the prestigious School of Cinema Arts at the University of Southern California so all was well that ended well, but I might have avoided my eight years as a drop-out if I'd had active and involved counseling.

"Then, as a parent of home schooled children, I worried a little about how to keep records, get tests, provide high school transcripts. I didn't know how it was done, there was no school that taught home school administration, but I did know how to learn so I got the necessary information as it was needed and we never had a problem. When my kids wanted to enroll in junior college courses they aced the English placement tests, though they were then pre-teens. When they needed a transcript, I created one.

"Three years ago, my two children and I all came down with a disabling neuro-immune disease and homeschooling became sick-schooling. Now my diminished learning ability centered on the illness and the search for treatment, and the children learned whatever they comfortably could in the course of being distracted from chronic pain. My younger child grew well enough to be active again, while I remained housebound and my older child bedridden. So the younger child is now attending a public high school, excelling, but wishing there were a program like SWAS.

"I wish it too, and I wish it for all children, especially as they hit their teens and feel the need both to run in a pack and to deviate from the norm. I remember SWASies boarding a bus at different stops in different colors of face paint, or riding to the shopping center in a grocery cart full of Jello, long before the term 'performance art' was invented. These things were more important to my life thereafter than algebra—though I got algebra too, as it happened. (Sorry Chris: I never loved it much: I only worked hard to pass algebra so I would feel okay about taking your Wilderness Experience cluster.) When I could work, I did public radio and living history, weird stuff, and I never forgot that I learned the word 'deviant' in SWAS.

"The project about which I recently contacted Kathlene Carney for publicity help was a public activism art project to call attention to the need for research and patient services, for this disease of ours: Myalgic Encephalomyelitis. Through activism I'm continuing, despite disabling illness, to learn and to teach. I push past boundaries: even those thrown up by microbes. I thank the teachers who taught me how to learn."

CHAPTER EIGHTEEN

LAST GENERAL MEETING: KATE BLICKHAHN

"What will they do now?" she wondered. Yes, their appearance and symbolic violence to themselves caused the hostile reactions they got on the main campus, but she felt a sudden kinship with them, a wailing of dread at having to leave the friendly acceptance and warmth at SWAS to face the pockets of meanness and intolerance across the bridge."

The following piece was written by Kate Blickhahn, a former district administrator and English teacher par excellence, who taught in SWAS during its final year. She describes the painful last meeting when we told the students that we were closing SWAS down. Although she has changed the names of the staff, it may be easy to tell who is who. I am grateful to have found this accurate and lovingly recorded account of a difficult meeting.

ANN FELT HER STOMACH muscles tighten as she followed students into the crowded, cluttered classroom. She glance around anxiously at the eighty or so teenagers already in the room; they were sprawled on the carpet, bunched together on the battered couches at the edge of the carpet, perched on tables, sitting in chairs, and lining the walls. She found a chair next to Mark who scratched his peppery beard and returned a rueful half-smile. As she folded her hands she noticed that they were sweating.

"I don't want to run this meeting," Randy said soberly. "Alex, come on up here." Ann was touched by the absence of his usual sunniness; he looked so old and tired. Although she understood his reluctance, she felt uneasy that he wasn't taking charge. After all, he was the faculty head of their small alternative school.

Had the five of them discussed strategy for this meeting? She tried to recall. She could remember the painstaking job of wording the announcement that SWAS, their School Within a School, would have to close. They had planned the meeting with their stunned Parent Support Group, But what had been decided about today? Shouldn't one of the five of them say something? It seemed so cold and shocking simply to hand out the dittoed announcement and let it go at that. Some of the students knew; the word had spread quickly after the parent meeting. Others obviously did not know and were reading the paper with gasps, moans, little cries.

There was an uncomfortable silence as Alex, the student chair, strode to the front of the room and stood, his hands thrust deep in his pockets of his combat fatigue pants.

"Anyone want to say anything?" he asked, shrugging his shoulders.

"I want to hear from the teachers," said Paul, his face furrowed and his voice tinged with hurt. "I don't understand any of this. Mark? Lee?"

Murmurs around the room echoed his question. He shifted for space on the desk in the back of the room, squeezing against other students and against the piles of books and papers, waiting for an answer.

"There's not much we can say except to try to go over the reasons on this paper," said Randy, fighting for control of his voice. Ann shifted with relief that at least things were underway.

"At last Thursday's orientation meeting, we only had eight students and their parents, and there were just two other applications. When the staff met on Friday, that fact just capped off other pressures we've been feeling. We knew we had to close." Nodding at Jack, the school's principal, he continued, "We met with Jack on Monday and he agreed we should make the decision now, while there was still time to make changes in the schedule on the main campus."

"But what do we do now?" wailed Sarah. Ann looked over at the small contingent of punk rock girls huddled at the edge of the spattered carpet, their identity proclaimed by their ragbag clothes, their multiple earrings and nose rings, their assorted garish and ghoulish makeup, their wild hair - the rainbow Mohawk, the bleached rooster comb, the black spikes. Ann knew that most of the students would blend in easily on the main campus, but these visible few, this so fragile group that helped continue the misconception that SWAS was a school for left-over hippies, punks and assorted weirdoes, "What *will* they do now?" she wondered. Yes, their appearance and symbolic violence to themselves caused the hostile reactions they got on the main campus, but she felt a sudden kinship with them, a wailing of dread at having to leave the friendly acceptance and warmth at SWAS to face the pockets of meanness and intolerance across the bridge. She remembered the recent barbed wire fence erected one night, and the sign, "Keep SWAS out!"

"I'm in shock," said Carol, "just total shock," as she strained forward out of the tangle of students on the floor.

Next to Ann, Ruth had alternately gasped, mumbled, moaned and finally cried out, "There is no way I can make it on the main campus, just no way," her hair curtaining her face as she hunched over the table. Ann reached over and put her arm around Ruth, tears welling up in her eyes as she compared this picture of misery to the joyous dancing girl who only short weeks before had showed off her accomplishment, becoming the youngest Sufi Whirling Dervish in the country.

Jim, his small athletic body balanced in one of the windows at the back of the room, shouted, "It seems totally unfair. It's like a divorce when one person just says I want a divorce and the other person has no idea that anything is wrong. Why didn't we know sooner so that we could have done something?"

"It does seem precipitous," snipped Katherine in her fake British accent as she peered sternly over her glasses.

Ann felt the sting of truth and chose her words carefully. "We know it does seem sudden. But the signs have been there all year if you think back. Remember all those meetings last fall about the homework crisis? Remember all our discussions in General Meeting and tribe meetings about the lack of energy, lack of commitment? You know how much trouble we have had getting a good turn-out for Tribe P.E. And remember the difficulty we had getting projects organized?" Ann heard the pleading in her voice, the hope that they would all begin to understand.

"But you never said anything about closing," said JoAnne accusingly. "What about all of us in the Outdoor Leadership Project when there is no Wilderness next year. It all seems like a total waste." She punched her hand.

"You'll find places to use what you have learned," said Lee, the faculty head of the Wilderness Project. Ann knew that she meant it, but somehow the assurance rang hollow.

"Can't we do something?" asked Carol in a high plaintive voice. "I just can't go back to all those cliques in the main school and those mean teachers." Can't we try to get more kids? I'll bet if we try really hard we could recruit enough. How many do we need? Fifty-five? I'll bet we could get fifty-five kids.

Lee, her commanding voice quieting the murmurs, said slowly, "Yes, we might be able to mount a huge recruiting effort. But that's not the point. We love all of you, and no one is to blame for what is happening. But there just isn't the spark anymore." She shifted her sturdy frame on the arm of the stuffed chair and continued, "Things have become too institutionalized. Everyone seems to expect the same old projects: Ashland, Wilderness, Vision Quest. I can clearly remember when the Bear valley run was created. A girl said, 'Hey, wouldn't it be neat if the whole school...' and the run was created. Now we have it twice a year and everyone moans, 'Oh God, the Bear Valley run. Do we have to?' and only half the people in each tribe show up."

She paused, and stared down at the floor. Ann agonized for her in her search for an explanation that wouldn't seem as if she were scolding. "Without more student creativity, the staff has had to do more of the planning; we struggle harder to get kids to take part in the activities which are the very glue of SWAS, the things that create family feeling. An you know how hard it is for us to cover in the math classes the same curriculum as the man campus when we only meet three days a week. We are all working too hard. The whole idea of SWAS was that it was to be a school where kids made decisions about – and took responsibility for – their education."

"That is the thing that makes this such a bummer," said Alex, stabbing the air with his index finger. "This is supposed to be a kid-run school, and we weren't even part of the decision. The process is all fucked up."

Ann heard Mark snort softly, and reflected on the irony that Alex had been labeled, by students and staff alike, as the biggest flake around. Randy had complained that he had neglected the simplest of his responsibilities in the Make It Happen class.

"Yeah, that's right," shouted Jerry, swinging up to the front with his fists clenched. "I think we could keep SWAS open. You aren't the only teachers around! I think we should keep the school open and get five new teachers." Ann glanced around, noting the juxtaposition of the hostile student faces against the painted mural of jungle animals around the capitol dome. She could feel the rising tide of resentment, hurt and blame.

From the other side of the room, Robert stomped to the center, clutching his guitar by its neck. Usually the Johnny Carson comic, the school's unofficial master of ceremonies, he glared, set his jaw and shouted, "I am so angry I don't know what to say. I love you all so much, but right now I feel like going out and putting sugar in your gas tanks."

"Let's start our own school," shouted Carol, shaking her fist, "How many of you want to fight this thing?" She turned on her knees to count the hands being raised uncertainly.

Ann saw Jack lean forward in his chair and sighed gratefully as he said quietly, "I know you are all angry and upset. But I think the staff made the right decision. You can certainly try to get some other teachers, and we can certainly explore other alternatives. But your chances of saving SWAS are very slim. You know I have supported this school for all four years that I have been here, but you just aren't going to find any finer, more dedicated, more cohesive a team than you have right here. If they say it is time to close, it is time to close."

Roy, a small, sharp-featured freshman, had been waving his hand, trying to say something. "I don't think you guys are approaching this right at all," he said in his usual curt, confident voice. "I think we should try to understand the staff's point of view. They are tired and the program isn't working like it used to. They thought a lot about the decision and I think we should support them and plan what to do next." Ann sent him a silent 'thank you' but felt the rebuff other students gave him in the glances and murmurs around the room. She could, though, feel the anger subsiding.

Mary, her fellow English teacher, sitting cross-legged on one of the tables behind Roy, reached out of her shawl and put a hand on his shoulder. "We understand that you feel angry, betrayed. It's okay to be mad. I'd be mad, too." She continues, "It's okay to be scared, too. I am scared about teaching French on the main campus. But a big part of me is kind of excited."

"But look at what we are losing," said Alice, crying quietly. "I feel like I am losing my family."

Ann felt a tightness in her chest at the sad echoes which rose around the room. Finally Randy got up slowly and looked around the room. "I think we've said all we can ay about this now. Let's have the teachers meet in my room, and if you want to stay here to talk more, that's fine." The teachers staggered out, most of the students remaining behind them.

"It's hard, isn't it?" said Randy, settling himself at a table in his room.

"Harder than anything," agreed Mary, pulling her shawl tightly around her.

"We know we've made the right decision, though," said Mark. "Does anyone really feel as if it's a mistake?"

"Boy, I don't know," sighed Lee, slumping dejectedly in her chair.

Ann thought, "But we do know," and remembered their shared fatigue, their discussions about how the range of students had narrowed in the past years, their confessions about other things they would like to explore. They had, even before they realized it, moved as a single organism toward what had to be done.

Suddenly Shane burst into the room. "Come on, you guys," he shouted. "We are going to get a picture of everyone."

Out in the hall, the tone had completely changed. Kids were crowding toward the front steps of the building, lining up in the traditional pose for the school picture. Ann laughed with relief, and watched as Randy got out this camera for this second school picture of the year. Kids were shouting, gathering everyone, arranging tables to make enough tiers on the porch. The five teachers linked arms and ran down the hall.

"We're going to be fine," thought Ann, as she smiled at the camera. And for the moment, that was a certainty.

CHAPTER NINETEEN

WHAT'S OLD IS NEW AGAIN

*Before there was Restorative Justice, SWAS had the Grievance
Committee; before anyone ever spoke the word Mindfulness,
Paul Ehrlich and I taught yoga to the whole school; before
anyone touted Project-Based Learning, we had semester-long
project groups; before the emphasis on building students' self-
esteem, we had weekly Support Groups; and before any focus on
Academies or the Small Schools Movement, we had ... SWAS.*

URRENT EDUCATIONAL RESEARCH FOCUSES on the benefit
of inquiry-based instruction, the use of Essential Questions, Small
Learning Communities and Project-based Learning. It makes me
smile that these ideas are often known by their initials: PBL, SLC, etc.
Even the most cursory glance into the research shows how closely the
ideas – and the results – align with those in the SWAS program. ERIC,
the Educational Resources Information Center, puts it this way: "In an age
of reform and restructuring, educators are seeking new models to improve
their schools. One approach is to replicate the qualities, and hopefully the
advantages, of a small school by creating a 'school-within-a-school.' This
approach establishes within the school a smaller educational unit with
a separate educational program, its own staff and students, and its own
budget. Several cities, including New York City, Philadelphia, and Chicago,
have experimented with this as a method for downsizing (Raywid, 1995)."
ERIC goes on to briefly introduce the school-within-a-school concept,

summarizing existing research on school-within-a-school models, and reviewing some of the advantages and disadvantages.

An old adage states: "Tell me and I forget, show me and I remember, involve me and I understand." The last part of this statement is the essence of inquiry-based learning now and was of SWAS then. In addition, the following description of Project-based Learning could have been used by the teachers who developed SWAS.

> Project-based learning (PBL) involves students in a model that encourages them to engage in learning activities that are long-term, interdisciplinary, and integrated with real-world issues and practices. The focus is a shift from short, isolated lessons where students have 40 minutes of math instruction followed by 40 minutes of science followed by 40 minutes of reading. In PBL students are using their skills and knowledge in a variety of subjects to solve problems and/or create products.

> PBL motivates children to engage in their own learning by creating a product that allows them to practice and demonstrate academic skills and knowledge. PBL makes learning meaningful and practical by fostering connections to the world outside the classroom/home.

> Learning is more authentic because students are given projects that are much more similar to those they will experience in a "real" work environment and in real world situations they encounter outside the classroom or home. Even at a young age children are able to practice and apply skills of scholars, researchers, and other professionals. For example, when a child is participating in a project he may be asked to develop a project plan, create a draft for the plan, get feedback on his ideas, possibly conduct research in an area(s), and finally prepare to share a product with an audience. Depending on the age and independence of the child, the parent or teacher provides the appropriate

support and structure to help the child accomplish some or all of these goals. Students are not only learning the skills associated with the subject areas, they are also learning social skills, life skills, self-management skills, and independence.

As a child engages in their project, the teacher or parent takes opportunities to have conversations about the student's ideas, provide feedback, encourage thought, and to discuss the learning that is taking place.

With project-based curriculum students feel "connected" to what they are doing. They experience a sense ownership and responsibility. As a summative experience, students are encouraged to share their projects with their family and friends. This gives the child a sense of accomplishment and pride that far outweighs any worksheet or test. (Alan Colburn, California State University, Long Beach California)

http://www.movingbeyondthepage.com/curriculum/ strategyprojectbasedinstruction.aspx

Theodore Sizer's work, *Horace's School* and *Horace's Compromise* present his reflection on a five-year study in which a team of investigators toured high schools of various kinds (differing demographic composition, rural and urban, public, private, and parochial), interviewed teachers, students, and administrators, and observed classes and followed students through their daily routines. Sizer criticizes the standard 50-minute classroom block used in scheduling, which he claimed limited the depth of any learning, and the over-use of elective courses.

His chief focus, however, is on specific practices of teaching and learning. Like John Dewey, Sizer insists that education must be a give-and-take interaction between teacher and student, where the teacher is the guide on the side rather than the sage on the stage.

The original principles that he emphasizes are:

Learning to use one's mind well
Less is More, depth over coverage
Goals apply to all students
Personalization
Student-as-worker, teacher-as-coach
Demonstration of mastery
A tone of decency and trust
Commitment to the entire school

Behind all of these models lies the recognition that the personalization possible within a smaller school setting is vital. The Educational Resource Information Center of the U.S. Department of Education reported in 2007 as follows:

> Large schools have implemented a myriad of programs to downsize or downscale: house plans, mini-schools, learning communities, clusters, charters, and schools-within-schools. Each model differs from the others on a range of factors, including how separate the subunit is from the larger institution and how much autonomy it receives to manage its own education program. The models also differ in terms of programs and organizational structure and practice (Raywid, 1995). Some simply group cohorts of students together while maintaining a symbolic and administrative identification with the larger school. The school-within-a-school model has the greatest levels of autonomy, separateness, and distinctiveness. Students follow a separate education program, have their own faculty, and identify with their sub-school unit. Because the school-within-a-school model replicates a small school more closely than the other forms of downsizing, it is most likely to produce the positive effects of small-scale educational organization.
>
> (http://www.education.com/reference/article/ Ref_School_within_School/)

This ERIC study concludes that a review of the literature suggests that implementing the school-within-a-school model has met with varying degrees of success in different settings. The most critical factor for success is a commitment to implementing the program fully, allowing for complete administrative separation of the school within a school and the creation of a separate identity (McCabe & Oxley, 1989; McMullan, Sipe, & Wolfe, 1994; Raywid, 1996b). Without full implementation, many of the benefits of small-scale schooling, such as establishing community and symbolic identity, cannot be realized. Staff and student support is also important, and the strengths or weaknesses of a particular plan may vary over the years with personnel changes. Obtaining the support of the superintendent, school board, and school principal is also essential. Our experience lead us to identical conclusions. While we did not have, or want, a separate administration, it was essential that we had a separate identity and were given autonomy in decision making.

The most important benefit of the sixteen years of SWAS in our eyes was the often-intangible one having to do with students' self-esteem, social connectedness and improved attitude about learning. Current research concurs.

> Greenleaf's research (1995) suggests that "creating learning communities for young people ... increased their social commitment to one another and to their teachers, thereby increasing their personal investments in school" (p. 46). Evidence related to educational achievement is less clear. Several studies provide evidence that school downsizing models can contribute to increased educational achievement and attainment (Crain, Heebner, & Si, 1992; McMullan, Sipe, & Wolfe, 1994; Robinson-Lewis, 1991). Some research, however, suggests that subschools produce only moderate or mixed gains in achievement (Robinson-Lewis, 1991; Jokiel & Starkey, 1972; Morriseau, 1975).

> http://www.ericdigests.org/2000-4/school.htm

The National Educational Association concluded that "an extensive amount of research indicates that there may be many benefits from smaller learning communities (Supovitz & Christman, 2005; Howley, et al., 2000). The most important benefits include:

- Raised student achievement
- Increased attendance
- Elevated teacher satisfaction,
- Improved school climate

In addition to the benefits listed above, research indicates that there may be improved instructional quality and working conditions. These factors also play a role in greater job satisfaction for the small school faculty (Darling-Hammond 2002).

A small school offers an environment in which students may be more visible. Student-teacher relationships improve, allowing teachers to more easily identify individual talents and unique needs of each student, which offers a more personalized educational experience. Teachers are able to interact more with their faculty administrators. A small school staff size allows more opportunity for teachers to know each other well, more easily share information about their students, collaborate to solve problems, and generally support one another." http://www.nea.org/home/13639.htm

Finally, with the recent attention put on the disastrous effects of bullying in schools, it is interesting to note that psychologists describe the difference between bullying and regular, normal kid-teasing, is that the bullied child feels isolated, and unable to communicate with anyone who might help. This is where a school-within-a-school can truly be most helpful - even live-saving - for that sense of community and connectedness engendered by this model means that no child feels alone, unseen or unheard. Some of the references citing studies about Schools-Within-Schools include these:

Cotton, K. (1996a). *School size, school climate, and student performance. Close-up #20. Portland, OR: Northwest Regional Educational Laboratory. (ERIC Document Reproduction Service No. ED 397 476)*

Cotton, K. (1996b). *Affective and social benefits of small-scale schooling.* ERIC Digest. Charleston, WV: ERIC Clearinghouse on Rural Education and Small Schools. (ERIC Document Reproduction Service No. ED 410 088)

Fowler, W. J., Jr. (1995). School size and student outcomes. In H. J. Walberg (Series Ed.) & B. Levin, W. J. Fowler, Jr., and H. J. Walberg (Vol. Eds.), *Advances in education productivity: Vol 5. Organizational influences on productivity* (pp. 3-25). Greenwich, CT: Jai Press.

Gordon, R. (1992). *School within a school: Grades 7, 8, 9, 10. Focus on program evaluation.* Des Moines, IA: Des Moines Pubic Schools. (ERIC Document Reproduction Service No. ED 371 045)

Greenleaf, C. L. (1995). *You feel like you belong: Student perspectives on becoming a community of learners.* Paper presented at the Annual Meeting of the American Educational Research Association, San Francisco.

Howley, C. B. (1994). *The academic effectiveness of small scale schooling (an update).* ERIC Digest. Charleston, WV: ERIC Clearinghouse on Rural Education and Small Schools. (ERIC Document Reproduction Service No. ED 389 503)

Lee, V. E., & Smith, J. B. (1995). Effects of high school restructuring and size on early gains in achievement and engagement. *Sociology of Education, 68(4),* 241-270.

Lee, V. E., & Smith, J. B. (1996). *High school size: Which works best, and for whom?* Paper presented at the Annual Meeting of the American Educational Research Association, New York.

McCabe, J. G., & Oxley, D. (1989). *Making big high schools smaller: A review of the implementation of the house plan in New York City's most troubled high schools.* New York: Public Education Association; Bank Street College of Education.

Moffett, J. J. (1981). *Options in secondary education: The school within a school concept.* Unpublished doctoral dissertation, University of Arizona.

Muncey, D. E., & McQuillan, P. J. (1991). School-within-a-school restructuring and faculty divisiveness: Examples from a study of the coalition of essential schools. Working Paper #6. Providence, RI: School Ethnography Project, Brown University.

Raywid, M. A. (1995). The subschools/small schools movement--taking stock. Madison, WI: Center on Organization and Restructuring of Schools. (ERIC Document Reproduction Service No. ED 397 490)

Raywid, M. A. (1996a). Taking stock: The movement to create mini-schools, schools-within-schools, and separate small schools. Urban Diversity Series No. 108. New York: ERIC Clearinghouse on Urban Education. Madison, WI: Center on Organization and Restructuring of Schools. (ERIC Document Reproduction Service No. ED 396 045)

Raywid, M. A. (1996b). The Wadleigh complex: A dream that soured. In W. Boyd, R. Crowson, & H. Mawhinney (Eds.), The politics of education and the new institutionalism: Reinventing the American school. Philadelphia: Falmer.

Googling the "School Within a School Movement" will lead you to myriad other resources and testimonials. Listening to NPR will bring report after report about new schools designed to focus on emotional intelligence, project-based learning and stress reduction. Three current films also come to mind. Greg Whitely's "Most Likely to Succeed" and two by Tom Valen's, "From August to June" and "Good Morning, Mission Hill," all document the success of alternative school models. Each film follows a class for a full year, Whitley's High Tech High School in San Diego and Valen's 4th grade Open Classroom in rural Lagunitas and Mission Hill in urban Boston. All three schools clearly measure success through project-based learning and the development of "soft skills" like confidence, time management and collaboration. Teachers are given complete freedom in the classroom, separate from state-mandated requirements such as standardized testing.

Some of the terms are new, but before there was Restorative Justice, SWAS had the Grievance Committee; before anyone ever spoke the word Mindfulness, Paul Ehrlich and I taught yoga to the whole school; before anyone touted Project-Based Learning, we had semester long project groups; before the emphasis on building students' self-esteem, we had weekly Support Groups; and before any focus on Academies or the Small Schools Movement, we had ... SWAS.

However, let's end with the voice of one last SWAS grad who said, "I don't have children of my own. However, watching a classmate's oldest boy at Drake leaves me with the feeling that SWAS perhaps didn't die away in 1984, but was slowly embedded into the main school over a couple decades. When I hear of his classes in the Drake High CORE Academy, all the trips they take and the focus on both critical and creative thinking and direct action, it seems as though he is perhaps, today, at a larger SWAS." We hope so, too.

Thank you to Juli Gicker and Kathleen Morgen, with whom the idea for this book first started.

Thank you to Rudy Genetti, Brad Nicholson, Chris Fulmer, Ken Genetti and the rest Rudy's photography students for the photographs, and to the Genetti family for permission to use them. Thanks to Mhana Mason and Cathy Reinhard for maintaining all those wonderful slides and for their help and support when I got discouraged. Special thanks to Jay Daniels at Black Cat Studios for rescanning the slides for this book.

It was Eilene Bundy who kept such careful notes of the early days of SWAS. Thank you to Chris Anderson, Jackie Moskowitz, Warren Fairbanks, Juli Gicker, Meegan Ochs Potter, Chris Fulmer, Bob Morgen, Martin Sirk, James Graham, Laurel Headley, Kyle Thayer, Ken Genetti, Dov Hassan, Kathleen Fatooh, Mhana Mason, Angela Hildebrand and Kate Blichkahn for their contributions to the text, and to Kyle Thayer and Keith Lester for skillful proof-reading and for their encouraging words. Thanks to Facebook for making connections easy over the years!

Lastly, I give my apologies to anyone I have neglected to thank. Each and every SWASie has contributed to this book and has made my life richer and me more grateful.

ABOUT THE AUTHOR

Martha Allen taught for over 36 years in Marin County at Sir Francis Drake High School, Redwood High School and Dominican University. Named Marin County Teacher of the Year, she continues to volunteer after retirement at her local elementary school.

Printed in the United States
By Bookmasters